600 Keto Diet Instant Pot Cookbook #2019

5 Ingredients Keto Diet Recipes, Keto Instant Pot Recipes with 21-Day Meal Plan for Your Instant Pot Pressure Cooker (Upgraded Edition)

By Jamie Michael

D1410866

Legal & Disclaimer

The information and contents herein are not designed to replace or take the place of any form of medical or professional advice and are not meant to replace the need for independent medical, financial, legal or other professional advice or services, as may be required. The content and information in this book have been provided for educational and entertainment purposes only.

The content and information in this book have been compiled from reliable sources and are accurate to the author's best knowledge, information, and belief. The author cannot guarantee this book's accuracy and validity and cannot be held liable for any errors and/or omissions. Further, changes will be periodically made to this book when needed. It is recommended that you consult with a health professional who is familiar with your personal medical history before using any of the suggested remedies, techniques, or information in this book.

Upon using the contents in this book, you agree to hold harmless the author from and against any damages, costs, and expenses, including any legal fees potentially resulting from the application of the information provided You agree to accept all risks associated with using the information presented inside this book.

Table of Content

Introduction

Are you struggling to find the best way to lose weight? Well, you can now sit and relax because that came to an end a few seconds ago. I am a living testimony that the Keto diet is the ultimate problem solver and is 100% effective.

If you last saw me two years ago, and you see me right now, you would be surprised that I am a totally different person in terms of my size. At that time, I have shed off about half of my weight.

I must say that it's not easy being overweight, or rather weighing way much more than the average person. To make you understand, let's do a flashback of me some years back.

"Alex, you are getting so fat." That was the statement from one of the girls in my class. Me? Fat? No way! "I am not fat," I tried to comfort myself. Honestly speaking, that statement struck me like a sword while deep down, I knew it was true.

I just had to do something immediately that would make me cut my weight. I decided to cut the "fatty" foods that I thought greatly contributed to my weight. I was in college when I noticed that I am becoming "overweight."

Fast-forward three months later, I got the shock of my life when I realized that instead of cutting my weight, I had gained two pounds. "How on earth did that happen?" I couldn't help but think that I had made such a joke of myself because the results were the opposite of what I expected. "There has to be a way out of this," I told myself.

In the process of finding a solution, my friend Kristen told me about the keto diet. He told me that her mom used that diet, and she lost her weight even without having to avoid "fatty" foods like me. That is the moment I made a decision that I will try this diet.

I must say that was the best decision I ever made in regards to my weight. I have managed to cut my weight while enjoying the delicious recipes that are keto. I wished I had earlier met someone to tell me about the amazing keto diet.

With the keto diet, there is a wide variety of meals that you can eat. There are snacks, appetizers, poultry, meat and also drinks. You will enjoy the best recipes while you lose weight effortlessly. Who wouldn't want that? I know you want it too. This is the reason why you should go for a ketogenic diet and enjoy its full benefits.

This book is the ultimate guide to the ketogenic diet. It has all the information that you need to know about keto. The recipes in this book are proven to work. I have cooked every one of them, and they are the reason I have cut a lot of weight. Try them and you will not regret it.

Thanks for downloading my book! Enjoy reading!

Chapter 1: Ketogenic Diet Explained

What is a ketogenic diet?

It is a low-carb, high-fat, and moderate protein diet. The main premise behind the keto diet is to make your body more efficient at using fat for fuel instead of sugar. When you're consuming a lot of carbohydrates, your body's blood sugar levels will spike up. Your body will then release a hormone called insulin to help regulate your blood sugar back down to normal.

History of the Ketogenic Diet

The ketogenic diet can trace to 1924 at the Mayo Clinic. A doctor by the name Russel Wilder realized that the symptoms of diabetic patients were less frequent when on a fast. They were on a diet consisting of carbohydrates and proteins in a ratio of 1:4. Foods with high carbohydrates were removed from the diet. These foods were sugar, fruits, pasta, grains and starchy vegetables.

This diet became popular in the control of epilepsy, but it reduced in the following decades due to the development of anticonvulsant drugs. Most healthcare givers and patients found it hard to strictly adhere to the ketogenic diet as opposed to administering pills, which was easier. However, some medical centers like the Johns Hopkins Medical used the ketogenic diet as the treatment option.

Interest on the ketogenic diet to manage epilepsy resurfaced in the mid-1990s. The son of Jim Abrahams, a film producer, had a seizure disorder and was put on the treatment of which the ketogenic diet was part of it. Adherence to the ketogenic diet controlled the seizures successfully. It is as a result of this success that the family founded the Charlie Foundation. The foundation was instrumental in funding ketogenic diet research. In 1997, a movie, First Do No Harm, was made and it created awareness about the ketogenic diet as a treatment method. There was renewed scientific interest in improving the ketogenic diet and other possible uses of the diet.

Why You Start the Ketogenic Diet

Increases HDL (Good Cholesterol)

The work of HDL is to carry cholesterol to the liver from the body so that it can either be excreted or reused. High levels of HDL can reduce the risk of heart disease. On a ketogenic diet, while consuming high amounts of fat, you will also ingest more "good" cholesterol.

Body Weight

Weight loss is one of the major reasons many people opt for a ketogenic diet. And studies have proved that it does allow greater weight reduction in a much easier way. It helps in losing weight and also helps to tone our muscles and body shape.

Reduces Blood Sugar and Insulin Levels

Carbohydrates raise sugar levels in the body. Having high blood sugar is toxic and causes insulin resistance, which leads to type 2 diabetes. A reduction in carbohydrate consumption leads to lower insulin and blood sugar levels. The ketogenic diet has been proved to improve health in diabetic subjects and reduce or eliminate the need for insulin.

Help with Skin Problems

For people having skin problems, especially acne, this diet is one good solution. In the absence of complex carbohydrates, there is the minimal production of toxins in the blood, thus keep our skin healthy and acne-free.

Blood Pressure

As the ketogenic diet helps to maintain high levels of triglyceride in the body, it is also effective in controlling blood pressure and cholesterol levels. This, in turn, saves us from many fatal diseases, like cardiovascular diseases.

Mental Focus

Ketones provide fuel for the brain. When carbohydrate intake is decreased, it eliminates blood sugar spikes. Together, these effects can improve concentration and focus. Studies have found that an increase in fatty acids can have a positive result on the overall function of the brain.

Reduces Hunger & Increases Energy

By providing your body with a more reliable source of energy, you will feel more energized throughout the day. When the body burns fats as fuel, they create the most energy for the body. Fat is more satisfying. It, therefore, makes satiated for a long period of time.

Epilepsy Treatment

Although the ketogenic diet has only recently gained public attention, it has been used since the 1900s as a successful treatment for epilepsy. The diet continues to be one of the most widely used therapies to treat children with uncontrollable epilepsy.

Food to Eat

Healthy Fats

- Saturated (goose fat, tallow, clarified butter/ghee, coconut oil, duck fat, lard, butter, chicken fat)
- Monounsaturated (olive, macadamia and avocado oil)
- Polyunsaturated omega 3s (seafood and fatty fish)

Non-Starchy Vegetables

- Spinach
- Endive
- Bamboo Shoots
- Asparagus
- Lettuce
- Cucumber
- Kale
- Radishes
- Celery Stalk
- Chives
- Zucchini
- ➢ Fruits like avocado, berries

Nuts And Seeds

Macadamia nuts, pine nuts, walnuts, sunflower seeds, sesame seeds, hemp seeds, pumpkin seeds, pecans, hazelnuts, almonds

Dairy Products

- Cream cheese
- Heavy whipping cream
- Whole milk yogurt (unsweetened)

Beverages

- Water
- Unsweetened herbal tea
- Unsweetened coconut milk
- Decaf coffee
- Unsweetened almond milk
- Unsweetened soy milk
- Unsweetened herbal tea

Protein

Fish: cod, halibut, tuna, salmon, trout, flounder, mackerel, snapper, and catfish.
Meat: Goat, Beef, Lamb, and other wild game
Poultry: Chicken meat, duck meat, and quail meat
Shellfish: Squid, Clams, scallops, shrimp, mussels, crab, and oysters,
Whole Eggs
Pork products
Sausage and bacon
Peanut Butter

Dressings

- Balsamic Vinegar
- Ranch
- Blue Cheese
- Apple Cider Vinegar
- Creamy Caesar

Spices

- Oregano
- Black Pepper
- Rosemary
- Basil
- Thyme
- Sea salt
- Cumin
- Parsley
- Sage
- Cayenne Pepper

Foods to Avoid

Processed Foods

Artificial sweeteners: sweeteners containing Aspartame, Equal, Sucralose, Acesulfame, Saccharin, Splenda

Refined fats/oils: grape seed, corn oil, sunflower

Alcoholic drinks: beer, cocktails,

Tropical fruit: papaya, banana, mango, pineapple

Weight Loss Tips

Keep Your Carbs Very Low

It is the most significant thing while on the keto diet. Maintaining your carbs low helps to get the body into ketosis.

Do not cheat as that will hinder your success and slow the process of your body adapting to ketosis. You make the decision yourself, and therefore, when you cheat, you are only doing it to yourself. Therefore, I advise you to never cheat during your keto journey.

Track Your Calories and Macros

Carbs are almost everywhere out there and you need to keep track of all that you eat.

Watch Your Electrolytes

Electrolytes are of great essence on a keto diet as they are removed from the body system.

Ensure that that you take enough potassium, magnesium and sodium to curb excessive hunger, cramps, water retention, headaches and cravings.

Be patient

Losing weight does not come overnight. You must consistently work hard over a long period of time to achieve this goal. A keto diet is an excellent diet if you want to lose weight.

However, you need to know that the weight cannot be lost in a fortnight. It may take you more than a month to notice a change in your weight.

Enough Sleep and Rest

Stress levels in a person are also a factor in losing weight. When you are more stressed, the level of cortisol increases, which in turn causes weight gain or retention.

Rest is also another very important factor. Most people require seven to nine hours of sleep for proper rest of the body each night.

Tips for Successful Ketogenic Journey

Clear Carbohydrates from Your Kitchen

Most people will only stick to the ketogenic diet if they had access to healthy ketogenic foods. This will help you a lot in avoiding falling prey to the carbohydrate concentrated foods in your cabinet. Clean your kitchen from high-carbohydrate foods like pastry, bread, potatoes, soda, rice, and candy. This will help a long way in achieving the ketogenic diet.

Have Ketogenic Snacks at Hand

Having to prepare a lot of homemade meals is a big challenge for people as regards the ketogenic diet. There is a solution for you: why not have ketogenic snacks instead whenever you are hungry and you are not at home?

You can buy ketogenic snacks like hard-boiled eggs, beef jerky, pre-cooked bacon, pre-made guacamole and so on, or you can have them on the go. You can prepare a lot of them and this will not allow you to buy carbohydrate-heavy snacks.

Buy a Food Scale

This might sound surprising but it is quite crucial. As it has been said, "Drops of water make an ocean." The amount of food you eat matters even to the tiniest form. Buy a food scale to measure your food and make sure you are eating the appropriate size because even the least can make a difference.

For example, 2 extra tablespoons of almond butter turn out to be an additional 200 calories and 6 grams of carbohydrates. It is not necessary you use the food scale until the end of your challenge. It is just for you to get the appropriate measurement, then you can eyeball to measure it as you continue.

Exercise Frequently

Exercising allows your body to break down the glycogen it has in store. It also helps you to get fit and healthy. It also helps you in maintaining your muscle mass and strengthens you.

Try Intermittent Fasting

This is one of the most effective tips that can get you right on track to achieving your fitness goals. It helps you get into ketosis and lose weight. This means that you do not eat anything that contains calories for a given period of time. A study at Harvard has made it known that intermittent fasting manipulates your mitochondria in a way that the ketogenic diet also does and this elongates your lifespan. When you stop taking calories for some time, your body will start breaking down the excess glucose in your body obtained from consuming carbohydrates.

Include Coconut Oil Into Your Diet

Coconut oil contains fats called medium-chain triglycerides which help you to get into ketosis quickly. Unlike other fats, the MCTs get absorbed rapidly into the liver where they can be used for energy or they can be converted into ketones.

Chapter 2: Understanding Instant Pot

What is an Instant Pot?

It is a multifunctional kitchen appliance that cooks fast, saving you time while at the same time retaining the nutritional values of your ingredients. It is automated and easy to use. It works as a warming pot, rice cooker, slow cooker and electric pressure cooker.

Advantages of Using an Instant Pot

Perfectly Cooked Meals

With the Instant Pot, you can make all types of perfectly cooked foods like pot roast in one pot. You can then "keep warm" using the 24-hour programmable timer. It spares you from using a skillet to brown your meat and sears in the juices. You won't need to be home to turn it to the "keep warm" setting after the cooking process is over, as the device will do that by itself. You can come home to perfectly cooked pot roast that is tender and succulent without falling apart into smithereens.

No Mess, Easy Clean

You have almost no mess to clean and wash after you are done with cooking because you have only used one pot for everything, which gets clean in no time.

Instant Pot comes with a removable stainless-steel inner cooking basket. Just simply remove it and place it in the dishwasher or rinse with soapy water. A simple wipe-down with a cloth on the outside and that's it. It spares you from heavy cleaning of your pots and pans.

Multifunctional

The Instant Pot can be used for many cooking functions. It can be used as a pressure cooker, slow cooker, warming pot and rice cooker. It is also used to bake and also make yogurt. This makes it an all-in-one appliance which saves you the need to buy other appliances.

Energy Efficient & Safe

Instant Pot is capable of cooking your foods fast using high-pressure steam and generating a high temperature; it can save up to 70% of electric consumption by taking less time to cook. It has been designed to concentrate energy only on cooking the added ingredients to prevent energy waste.

Space Saving

If you are always fighting for the space

Main Functions of the Instant Pot

Instant Pot allows you to prepare different types of foods. It offers all the basic as well as advanced cooking functions. Following are the advanced cooking functions offered by almost all Instant Pot models.

Adjust: This button allows you to change the temperature setting and time setting as per your needs.

Sauté: You can use this function to sauté or simmer your food such as onions, garlic, etc. with its lid open. This setting is also used to thicken the sauces.

in your kitchen, then Instant Pot is for you. Since you can pressure cook, slow cook, sauté, and brown along with multiple cooking settings mentioned earlier, you don't need to purchase multiple utensils as owning Instant Pot only is just enough. Its compact design takes less space and you can easily store it in your kitchen cabinet or countertop.

Food Retains More Nutrients

When pressure cooking, heat is distributed more evenly, and less water is used in the processing, so nutrients are not leached away. Not only does food retain its nutrients, but it also retains its color. Green beans stay green instead of turning gray. And the texture is much more appealing; no soggier, mushy vegetables!

Manual: This function allows you to customize the cooking time and temperature.

Steam: Usually used with a trivet, this function allows you to make all types of steamed dishes such as steamed vegetables, fish, and other seafood. The default cooking setting for this particular function is high pressure for 10 minutes.

Keep Warm/Cancel: Allows you to cancel the current cooking mode. It automatically sends the cooker in a standby mode and keeps the food warm.

Multigrain: Used to cook grains, brown rice, wild rice, and beans. The default cooking setting for this particular function is high pressure for 40 minutes.

Bean/Chili: This function allows you to cook bean dishes of your choice. The default cooking setting for this particular function is high pressure for 30 minutes.

Meat/ Stew: This function allows you to cook different types of meats and stews. The default cooking setting for this particular function is high pressure for 35 minutes.

Yogurt: This function allows you to turn the

8

Instant Pot into a yogurt maker. The default cooking setting for this particular function is 8 hours. But you can use the "Adjust" function to increase or decrease time.

Rice: This is the rice cooker mode. Use "Adjust" button to increase or decrease the cooking time.

Poultry: Cook different types of poultry meals with this function. Poultry meat is generally lighter and faster to cook than other types of meat. The default cooking setting for this particular function is high pressure for 15 minutes.

Soup: This function is great for cooking soups, stews, broths, and chowders. The default cooking setting for this particular function is high pressure for 30 minutes.

Porridge: It allows you to cook rice as well as other grains. The default cooking setting for this particular function is high pressure for 20 minutes.

Slow Cook: This function allows you to turn the device into a slow cooker. You can cook from 30 minutes to 20 hours with this function. You can delay cooking time up to 24 hours.

Cake: This function is for making a variety of cakes.

Egg: This function is for making a variety of egg-based recipes.

NPR (Natural Pressure Release): This setting is used for releasing the pressure naturally. It usually takes 8-15 minutes to release all the build-up pressure.

QPR (Quick Pressure Release): This setting is used for manually releasing the pressure quicker than it is released naturally by using the vent valve. Use a towel to cover the vent for better safety.

Cleaning the Instant Pot Pressure Cooker

As every electrical appliance needs constant care and maintenance, so does the instant pot pressure cooker. To ensure your personal safety, check all of its components at least once in a week. Regular maintenance will add up to the life of your cooker and will regulate its functionality.

It is recommended that the product should be cleaned after each use. As instant Pot consists of several different units, each part should be cleaned with extreme care.

1. Never clean the instant Pot immediately after cooking. Unplug the appliance first, let it cool for 30 minutes, and then start the cleaning process.

2. The black inner housing rim has to be wiped using a piece of cloth. Avoid washing, as it can cause rusting of the exterior pot rim.

3. To clean the inner Pot: First, remove the lid and take the Pot out. Now wash it with any detergent or soap then rinse with clear water. Use a soft cloth to wipe dry the inner Pot from inside out.

4. Wash the lid along with the sealing ring, anti-block shield, and exhaust valve with clear water. Wipe them dry using a soft cloth.

5. While washing the lid, make sure to leave the steam release pipe intact and do not remove it from the lid.

6. To clean the base unit: Remember not to immerse it completely in water. Use a wet cloth to wipe all the dirt out of it. Make sure that the device is completely unplugged while you are cleaning its Pot.

7. To clean the power plug and the cord: Always use a dry brush to remove the dirt or dust from the surface.

Instant Pot Frequently Asked Questions

1. Is the Instant Pot the Same as a Pressure Cooker?

No, it is not the same. While a pressure cooker only pressure cooks, the Instant Pot is a cooker with many functions like a pressure cooker, slow cooker, warming pot and rice cooker.

2. What are the Disadvantages of Using Instant Pot to Cook?

The main disadvantage is that you cannot adjust, taste or inspect the food when the cooking process starts. You have to wait for the set time to elapse.

3. Can I Pressure Fry with My Instant Pot?

Pressure frying is not recommended for electric pressure cookers because the splattering oil may melt the cooker gasket.

4. Is It Safe to Use the Instant Pot?

Yes, the Instant Pot is very safe to use. It has passed many UL certifications on safety.

5. Is the Cooking Process Faster When Using Instant Pot?

Using pressure to cook will always save you time. However, in some foods such as shrimps and broccoli, you may not notice this. When cooking foods such as pork, you will notice that time is significantly cut.

6. Can I Pressure-Can Using the Instant Pot?

No. There have been no tests carried on the Instant Pot on food safety in pressure canning.

7. What is the Working Pressure of the Instant Pot?

It ranges from 10.15-11.6 psi.

8. What are the Accessories You Recommend for Instant Pot?

Some of the recommended accessories include a steaming rack, meat thermometers, steamer baskets etc.

9. What Should I Do First After Just Getting My Instant Pot?

Before cooking, do a test run for the Instant Pot.

10. How Do I Use Quick Release?

When cooking is finished, unseal the venting knob to the venting position. It will take just a short time (usually a few minutes) for the pressure to be released.

11. How Do I Use Natural Release?

When cooking is finished, you wait for the valve to drop completely prior to opening the cover. Turn the knob to vent and the pressure will be released. It takes 10- 25 minutes.

Chapter 3 Breakfast Recipes

Mexican Egg Casserole

Prep Time + Cook time:30 minutes , Servings: 8

Ingredients:
- 1 pound ground pork sausage
- 1 small yellow onion, chopped
- 8 large eggs
- 1 cup diced red peppers
- 1 ½ cups shredded Mexican blend cheese

What you'll need from the store cupboard:
- ¼ cup coconut flour

Directions:
1. Turn the Instant Pot on to the Sauté setting and let it heat up.
2. Add the sausage and onion and cook until the sausage is browned about 5 minutes.
3. Whisk together the eggs and coconut flour, then pour into the pot.
4. Stir in the chopped peppers and Mexican cheese, then close and lock the lid.
5. Press the Manual button and adjust the timer to 20 minutes.
6. When the timer goes off, let the pressure vent naturally.
7. When the pot has depressurized, open the lid.
8. Remove the casserole to a plate and let rest 5 minutes before serving.

Nutrition:
calories 375 fat 28g , protein 23g , carbs 7g , fiber 3g , net carbs 4g

Sausage and Broccoli Egg Casserole

Prep Time + Cook time:45 minutes , Servings: 6

Ingredients:
- 8 ounces ground breakfast sausage
- 1 ½ cups grated broccoli
- 6 large eggs
- 1 cup shredded cheddar cheese
- Salt and pepper to taste

What you'll need from the store cupboard:
- 1 tablespoon olive oil
- 2 cloves minced garlic
- ¼ cup heavy cream

Directions:
1. Turn the Instant Pot on to the Sauté setting and let it heat up.
2. Meanwhile, grease a small casserole dish that can fit in the pot using cooking spray.
3. Heat the oil then add the sausage and cook until browned about 5 minutes, breaking it up with a spoon.
4. Stir in the grated broccoli and garlic then season with salt and pepper.
5. Cook for 2 to 3 minutes then spoon the mixture into the casserole dish.
6. Whisk together the eggs, cream, and cheese then pour into the casserole dish.
7. Cover the dish with foil and place it in the pot on top of a trivet.
8. Pour in one cup of water then close and lock the lid.
9. Press the Manual button and adjust the timer to 35 minutes.
10. When the timer goes off, let the pressure vent for 10 minutes then do a Quick Release by pressing Cancel and switching the steam valve to "venting."
11. When the pot has depressurized, open the lid.

12. Remove the casserole from the pot and let it rest for 10 minutes before slicing.

Nutrition:

calories 315 fat 25.5g ,protein 18.5g ,carbs 2.5g ,fiber 0.5g ,net carbs 2g

Sausage Gravy

Prep Time + Cook time:10 minutes , Servings: 6

Ingredients:

- 1 pound ground pork sausage
- ½ cup chicken broth
- 3 cups whole milk
- 6 tablespoons coconut flour

What you'll need from the store cupboard:

- Salt and pepper

Directions:

1. Turn the Instant Pot on to the Sauté setting and let it heat up.
2. Add the sausage and cook until browned, breaking it up into pieces.
3. Pour in the chicken broth, then close and lock the lid.
4. Press the Manual button and adjust the timer to 5 minutes.
5. When the timer goes off, do a Quick Release by pressing Cancel and switching the steam valve to "venting."
6. When the pot has depressurized, open the lid.
7. Whisk together the milk and coconut flour, then stir into the pot.
8. Cook on Sauté mode for 5 minutes until the sausage is thick.
9. Season with salt and pepper, then serve over keto biscuits.

Nutrition:

calories 375 fat 26g ,protein 20g ,carbs 13.5g ,fiber 5g ,net carbs 8.5g

Easy Eggs in a Jar

Prep Time + Cook time:10 minutes , Servings: 4

Ingredients:

- 4 large eggs
- ½ cup diced yellow onion
- ½ cup diced mushrooms
- ½ cup shredded cheddar cheese
- 2 cups of water

What you'll need from the store cupboard:

- Salt and pepper
- ¼ cup heavy cream

Directions:

1. Whisk together the eggs, onions, mushrooms, cheese, and heavy cream in a bowl.
2. Season with salt and pepper then pour into four ½-pint jars.
3. Place the lids loosely on top of the jars and place them in the Instant Pot on a trivet.
4. Pour in 2 cups of water then close and lock the lid.
5. Press the Manual button and adjust the timer to 5 minutes on High Pressure.
6. When the timer goes off, do a Quick Release by pressing Cancel and switching the steam valve to "venting."
7. When the pot has depressurized, open the lid.
8. Remove the jars from the Instant Pot and serve the eggs immediately.

Nutrition:

calories 165 fat 12.5g ,protein 10.5g ,carbs 2.5g ,fiber 0.5g , net carbs 2g

Cheesy Cauliflower and Ham Casserole

Prep Time + Cook time:35 minutes , Servings: 6

Ingredients:

- 8 ounces diced ham
- 1 ½ cups grated cauliflower
- 6 large eggs
- 1 cup shredded mozzarella cheese
- Salt and pepper to taste

What you'll need from the store cupboard:

- 1 tablespoon olive oil
- 2 cloves minced garlic
- ¼ cup heavy cream

Directions:

1. Turn the Instant Pot on to the Sauté setting and let it heat up.
2. Meanwhile, grease a small casserole dish that can fit in the pot using cooking spray.
3. Heat the oil then add the grated cauliflower and garlic. Season with salt and pepper.
4. Cook for 2 to 3 minutes then stir in the diced ham and spoon the mixture into the casserole dish.
5. Whisk together the eggs, cream, and cheese then pour into the casserole dish.
6. Cover the dish with foil and place it in the pot on top of a trivet.
7. Pour in one cup of water then close and lock the lid.
8. Press the Manual button and adjust the timer to 30 minutes.
9. When the timer goes off, let the pressure vent for 10 minutes then do a Quick Release by pressing Cancel and switching the steam valve to "venting."
10. When the pot has depressurized, open the lid.
11. Remove the casserole from the pot and let it rest for 10 minutes before slicing.

Nutrition:

calories 190 fat 13g ,protein 14.5g ,carbs 4g ,fiber 1g ,net carb 3g

Easy Spinach and Tomato Frittata

Prep Time + Cook time:10 minutes , Servings: 4

Ingredients:

- 6 large eggs
- 1 cup fresh chopped spinach
- ½ cup diced tomatoes
- 2 tablespoons diced yellow onion

What you'll need from the store cupboard:

- Salt and pepper
- ½ teaspoon garlic powder

Directions:

1. Whisk together all of the ingredients.
2. Pour the mixture into a greased 7-inch springform pan.
3. Place the pan in the Instant Pot on top of a trivet.
4. Pour in 1 cup of water then close and lock the lid.
5. Press the Manual button and adjust the timer to 5 minutes.
6. When the timer goes off, let the pressure vent for 10 minutes then do a Quick Release by pressing Cancel and switching the steam valve to "venting."
7. When the pot has depressurized, open the lid.
8. Remove the pan from the pot and let the frittata rest for 5 minutes before serving.

Nutrition:

calories 115 fat 7.5g ,protein 10g ,carbs 2.5g ,fiber 0.5g ,net carbs 2g

Bacon, Cheese, and Veggie Egg Bake

Prep Time + Cook time:30 minutes , Servings: 4

Ingredients:

- 6 slices bacon, chopped
- 1 cup chopped cauliflower
- ½ cup diced mushrooms
- 6 large eggs
- ½ cup shredded cheddar cheese

What you'll need from the store cupboard:

- Salt and pepper
- ¼ cup heavy cream
- 1 ½ cups water

Directions:

1. Turn the Instant Pot on to the Sauté setting and let it heat up.
2. Add the bacon and cook until crisp.
3. Stir in the vegetables and cook for 3 minutes, often stirring, until tender.
4. Grease a heatproof bowl with cooking spray.
5. Whisk together the eggs, cheese, and cream then season with salt and pepper.
6. Pour the egg mixture into the greased bowl then stir in the bacon and veggies.
7. Place the bowl in the pot on top of a trivet and pour in 1 ½ cups water.
8. Close and lock the lid then press the Manual button and adjust the timer to 20 minutes.
9. When the timer goes off, do a Quick Release by pressing Cancel and switching the steam valve to "venting."
10. When the pot has depressurized, open the lid.
11. Remove the bowl and turn the egg bake out and slice to serve.

Nutrition:

calories 275 fat 21g ,protein 19g ,carbs 3g ,fiber 1g ,net carbs 2g

Mediterranean-Style Frittata

Prep Time + Cook time:10 minutes , Servings: 4

Ingredients:

- 6 large eggs
- 1 cup fresh chopped spinach
- ½ cup diced tomatoes
- ½ cup feta cheese, crumbled
- ¼ cup sliced black olives

What you'll need from the store cupboard:

- Salt and pepper
- ½ teaspoon dried Italian seasoning

Directions:

1. Whisk together all of the ingredients.
2. Pour the mixture into a greased pan that fits in the pot.
3. Place the pan in the Instant Pot on top of a trivet.
4. Pour in 1 cup of water then close and lock the lid.
5. Press the Manual button and adjust the timer to 5 minutes.
6. When the timer goes off, let the pressure vent for 10 minutes then do a Quick Release by pressing Cancel and switching the steam valve to "venting."
7. When the pot has depressurized, open the lid.
8. Remove the pan from the pot and let the frittata rest for 5 minutes before serving.

Nutrition:

calories 175 fat 12.5g ,protein 12.5g ,carbs 3g ,fiber 1g ,net carbs 2g

Cheddar, Ham, and Chive Egg Cups

Prep Time + Cook time:10 minutes , Servings: 4

Ingredients:

- 4 large eggs
- ½ cup diced yellow onion
- ½ cup diced ham
- 2 tablespoons chopped chives
- ½ cup shredded cheddar cheese

What you'll need from the store cupboard:

- Salt and pepper
- ¼ cup heavy cream

Directions:

1. Whisk together the eggs, onions, ham, cheese, chives, and heavy cream in a bowl.
2. Season with salt and pepper then pour into four ½-pint jars.
3. Place the lids loosely on top of the jars and place them in the Instant Pot on a trivet.
4. Pour in 2 cups of water then close and lock the lid.
5. Press the Manual button and adjust the timer to 5 minutes on High Pressure.
6. When the timer goes off, do a Quick Release by pressing Cancel and switching the steam valve to "venting."
7. When the pot has depressurized, open the lid.
8. Remove the jars from the Instant Pot and serve the eggs immediately.

Nutrition:
calories 190 fat 14g ,protein 13g ,carbs 3g ,fiber 0.5g ,net carbs 2.5g

Garlic Spinach Omelet

Prep Time + Cook time: 20 minutes , Servings: 4

5-Ingredients:

- 6 whisked eggs
- 1 cup baby spinach
- 1 minced spring onion
- 1 cup water

What you'll need from the store cupboard:

- Cooking spray
- ½ tsp garlic powder
- A pinch of salt and black pepper

Directions:

1. Whisk the eggs, garlic powder, spinach, salt, and black pepper, and spring onions together in a bowl.
2. Coat the pan with the cooking spray and pour in the omelet mix.
3. Pour some water inside the instant pot and put the inner pot in and add the pan with the omelet mix inside the pot and seal the lid to cook for 10 minutes at high pressure.
4. Natural release the pressure for 10 minutes, share the omelet and serve.

Nutrition
Calories 103, fat 6.4, carbs 2.5, protein 8.4, fiber 1.1

Creamy Broccoli Pot Pie

Prep Time + Cook time: 50 minutes , Servings: 4

5-Ingredients:

- 3 Grated broccoli stalks
- 4 Whisked eggs
- 1 Chopped green onion
- ¼ cup Heavy cream
- 1 cup Grated cheddar cheese

What you'll need from the store cupboard:

- 2 tbsp Avocado oil
- A pinch of salt and black pepper
- 2 Minced garlic cloves

Directions:
1. Press 'Sauté' on the instant pot and pour the avocado oil into the pot and add the broccoli and garlic to 'Sauté' for 4 minutes.
2. Whisk the eggs, salt and pepper, and the cream in a bowl and pour it over the broccoli and garlic in the pot.
3. Seal the lid and set to cook for 35 minutes at high pressure.
4. Natural release the pressure for 10 minutes and drizzle the cheddar cheese and the green onions over it. Set aside for some minutes and serve into plates.

Nutrition
Calories 247, fat 19, carbs 2.3, protein 15, fiber 0.5

Cheesy Cauliflower Rice with Olives And Bell Peppers

Prep Time + Cook time: 25 minutes , Servings: 4

5-Ingredients:
- 1 cup Shredded cheddar cheese
- 2 cups Cauliflower; riced
- 1 cup Black olives; pitted and chopped
- 1 tsp Chopped red bell pepper
- 1 tsp Chopped green bell pepper

What you'll need from the store cupboard:
- A pinch of salt and black pepper
- ½ tbsp Olive oil

Directions:

1. Press 'Sauté' on the instant pot and pour the oil into it to heat it then add the cauliflower rice to cook for 2-3 minutes.
2. Mix in the remaining ingredients then seal the lid to cook for 12 minutes at high pressure.
3. Natural release the pressure for 10 minutes, then share into plates and serve.

Nutrition
Calories 199, fat 14.9, carbs 7.6, protein 8.9, fiber 3

Cheesy Paprika Broccoli and Scallions

Prep Time + Cook time: 30 minutes , Servings: 4

5-Ingredients:
- 1 lb. Broccoli florets: roughly chopped
- 1 cup Shredded cheddar cheese
- 2 Chopped scallions
- 4 Whisked eggs

What you'll need from the store cupboard:
- 1 tbsp Avocado oil
- 1 tbsp Sweet paprika

Directions:
1. Press 'Sauté' on the instant pot and add the oil. When hot, mix in the broccoli and the scallions to cook for 5 minutes.
2. Add the sweet paprika and the eggs, then seal the lid and cook for 15 minutes at high pressure.
3. Natural release the pressure for 10 minutes, drizzle the cheddar cheese over it and share it into plates to serve.

Nutrition
Calories 227, fat 14.8, carbs 6.7, protein 16, fiber 4

Cheesy Eggs and Bacon

Prep Time + Cook time: 25 minutes , Servings: 4

5-Ingredients:
- 1 Chopped shallot
- 1 cup Almond milk
- 1 ½ cups Chopped bacon
- 4 Whisked eggs
- 2 cups Shredded cheddar cheese

What you'll need from the store cupboard:
- A pinch of salt and black pepper
- 1 tsp Avocado oil

Directions:

1. Press 'Sauté' on the instant pot and add the oil. When hot, mix in the shallot and bacon to cook for 2-3 minutes.
2. Mix in the cheddar cheese, eggs, milk, salt, and pepper and seal the lid to cook for 12 minutes at high pressure.
3. Natural release the pressure for 10 minutes, share into plates and serve.

Nutrition
Calories 392, fat 37, carbs 4.6, protein 21, fiber 37

Cheesy Broccoli Cake

Prep Time + Cook time: 35 minutes , Servings: 4

5-Ingredients:
- 1 cup Grated broccoli florets
- 3 Whisked eggs
- 1 cup Shredded mozzarella
- 2 cups Coconut flour
- 1 Almond milk

What you'll need from the store cupboard:
- A pinch of salt and black pepper
- 1 tsp Baking soda
- Cooking spray

Directions:
1. Whisk the eggs with the flour, the salt and black pepper, broccoli florets, shredded mozzarella, baking soda, and almond milk in a bowl.
2. Coat the instant pot with the cooking spray and pour in the pancake mix. Seal the lid to cook for 25 minutes on high pressure.
3. Natural release the pressure for 10 minutes, then share the pancake into plates and serve.

Nutrition
Calories 76, fat 4.8, carbs 2, protein 6.8, fiber 0.6

Spinach and Tomatoes Jumble

Prep Time + Cook time: 20 minutes , Servings: 4

5-Ingredients:
- 3 cups Chopped baby spinach
- 1 lb. Mixed bell peppers; cut into strips
- 3 Chopped green onions
- 1 tbsp Olive oil
- 1 lb. Cubed cherry tomatoes

What you'll need from the store cupboard:
- A pinch of salt and black pepper
- 1 tbsp Balsamic vinegar

Directions:
1. Press 'Sauté' on the instant pot and add the oil. When hot, add the onions to brown for 2 minutes.
2. Mix in the tomatoes and the spinach, salt and pepper, green onions, vinegar, and bell peppers. Seal the lid to cook for 8 minutes on high pressure.

3. Natural release the pressure for 10 minutes, then share into plates and serve.

Nutrition

Calories 60, fat 8.1, carbs 6.1, protein 1.9, fiber 2

Creamy Chilies Omelet

Prep Time + Cook time: 40 minutes , Servings: 4

5-Ingredients:

- 4 Whisked eggs
- 1 tbsp Chopped cilantro
- ½ tsp Sweet paprika
- 1 cup Heavy cream
- 10 oz Canned green chilies

What you'll need from the store cupboard:

- A pinch of salt and black pepper
- 1 tbsp Avocado oil
- 1 tsp Chili powder

Directions:

1. Whisk the eggs with the cream, cilantro, chili powder, green chilies, salt and black pepper, and sweet paprika in a bowl.
2. Coat the instant pot with cooking oil and gently pour in the eggs mix then seal the lid to cook for 30 minutes on high pressure.
3. Natural release the pressure for 10 minutes, share into plates and serve.

Nutrition

Calories 404, fat 20.2, carbs 11.1, protein 14.6, fiber 8.9

Chili Asparagus and Eggs

Prep Time + Cook time: 25 minutes , Servings: 6

5-Ingredients:

- 1 halved Asparagus stalk
- 6 Whisked eggs
- 1 Chopped red chili pepper
- ¼ cup Chopped scallions

What you'll need from the store cupboard:

- A pinch of salt and black pepper
- 1 tbsp Olive oil
- ¼ tsp Chili powder

Directions:

1. Press 'Sauté' on the instant pot and add the oil. When hot, mix in the scallions and asparagus stalk to cook for 2-3 minutes.
2. Mix in the remaining ingredients and seal the lid to cook for 15 minutes at high pressure.
3. Quick-release the pressure for 5 minutes, share into plates and serve.

Nutrition

Calories 85, fat 6.7, carbs 0.8, protein 5.6, fiber 0.2

Almonds And Blueberries With Chia Bowls

Prep Time + Cook time: 15 minutes , Servings: 4

5-Ingredients:

- 2 tbsp Stevia
- ¼ cup Chia seeds
- 1 cup Blueberries
- 1/3 cup Chopped almonds
- 1 ½ cup Almond milk

What you'll need from the store cupboard:

- 1 tsp Vanilla extract

Directions:

1. Mix all the ingredients in the instant pot and seal the lid to cook for 10 minutes at high pressure.
2. Quick-release the pressure for 5 minutes, share into bowls and serve.

Nutrition
Calories 70, fat 4.1, carbs 4.2, protein 2, fiber 1.9

Creamy Cinnamon Strawberry Bowls

Prep Time + Cook time: 20 minutes , Servings: 4
5-Ingredients:
- 3 cups Almond milk
- 2 cups Strawberries; halved
- 1 tsp Cinnamon powder
- 2 ½ tbsp Cocoa powder
- ½ cup Coconut cream

What you'll need from the store cupboard:
- 1 tsp Vanilla extract

Directions:

1. Mix all the ingredients in the instant pot and seal the lid to cook for 10 minutes at high pressure.
2. Natural release the pressure for 10 minutes, share into bowls and serve.

Nutrition
Calories 312, fat 14.5, carbs 7.9, protein 5.6, fiber 4.6

Creamy Cinnamon Coconut Mix

Prep Time + Cook time: 10 minutes , Servings: 2
5-Ingredients:
- 1 cup Coconut milk
- ½ cup Unsweetened and flaked coconut
- 1 cup Yogurt
- ½ tsp Cinnamon powder
- ½ tsp Stevia

What you'll need from the store cupboard:
- ¼ tsp Vanilla extract

Directions:

1. Mix all the ingredients in the instant pot and seal the lid to cook for 5 minutes at high pressure.
2. Quick-release the pressure for 5 minutes, serve the creamy mix into bowls and serve.

Nutrition
Calories 218, fat 18.4, carbs 6.7, protein 5.2, fiber 2.2

Spicy And Creamy Artichokes Mousse

Prep Time + Cook time: 25 minutes , Servings: 4
5-Ingredients:
- 1 tbsp Chopped chives
- 2 cups Almond milk
- 1 ½ cups Canned artichokes; drained and chopped
- 1 tsp Sweet paprika
- ¼ cup Coconut cream

What you'll need from the store cupboard:
- A pinch of salt and black pepper

Directions:
1. Mix all the ingredients in the instant pot and seal the lid to cook for 15 minutes at high pressure.
2. Natural release the pressure for 10 minutes, share into plates and serve.

Nutrition
Calories 312, fat 23.4, carbs 7.3, protein 3.2, fiber 3.2

Spicy Pork In Tomato Sauce

Prep Time + Cook time: 24 minutes , Servings: 4

5-Ingredients:

- 1 lb. Ground pork
- 4 hard boiled and peeled Eggs
- 1 tsp Chopped cilantro
- 1 tsp hot paprika
- 1 cup Tomato passata

What you'll need from the store cupboard:

- A pinch of salt and black pepper
- 1 tbsp Avocado oil

Directions:

1. Combine the pork with cilantro, paprika, salt, and pepper in a bowl.
2. Mold into 4 balls and roll them out on a flat surface.
3. Put 1 egg on each rolled out pork mix and cover it with the mix.
4. Press 'Sauté' on the instant pot and add the oil. When hot, put the eggs in the oil to brown for 4 minutes all around.
5. Pour in the tomato passata, seal the lid and set to cook for 12 minutes at high pressure.
6. Quick-release the pressure for 6 minutes, share into plates and serve.

Nutrition

Calories 245, fat 8.9, carbs 3.9, protein 36, fiber 1.1

Cheesy Creamy Pork Pot Pie

Prep Time + Cook time: 40 minutes , Servings: 4

5-Ingredients:

- 1 cup Shredded cheddar cheese
- 4 Whisked eggs
- 2 Chopped green onions
- 2 cups Pork meat: ground and browned
- ½ cup Heavy cream

What you'll need from the store cupboard:

- A pinch of salt and black pepper
- 1 cup of water

Directions:

1. Whisk the eggs with the heavy cream, shredded cheese, pinch of salt and pepper, green onions, and pork meat in a bowl and pour it into a pie pan.
2. Pour the 1 cup of water into the instant pot and put in the inner pot then seal the lid to cook for 30 minutes on high pressure.
3. Natural release the pressure for 10 minutes, share into plates and serve.

Nutrition

Calories 231, fat 19.3, carbs 1.7, protein 13, fiber 0.2

Cinnamon Cauliflower Mousse

Prep Time + Cook time: 25 minutes   , Servings: 4

5-Ingredients:

- 2 cups Almond milk
- 1 cup Cauliflower rice
- 1 tsp Cinnamon powder
- 3 tbsp Stevia

What you'll need from the store cupboard:

- 1 tsp Vanilla extract
- 1 tbsp Grated ginger

Directions:

1. Combine all the ingredients in the instant pot and seal the lid to cook for 15 minutes on high pressure.

20

2. Natural release the pressure for 10 minutes. Mix the mousse, share it into bowls and serve.

Nutrition
Calories 284, fat 28.7, carbs 7.7, protein 2.9, fiber 2.8

Spicy Bok Choy And Tomatoes Soup Bowls

Prep Time + Cook time: 30 minutes , Servings: 4

5-Ingredients:
- 1 ½ cups Veggie stock
- 2 cups Roughly torn Bok Choy
- 2 Tomatoes: cubed
- 1 tbsp Sweet paprika
- 1 tbsp Coconut aminos

What you'll need from the store cupboard:
- A pinch of salt and black pepper
- 2 tbsp Grated ginger
- 2 Minced garlic cloves

Directions:
1. Combine all the ingredients in the instant pot and seal the lid to cook for 20 minutes at high pressure.
2. Natural release the pressure for 10 minutes, share into bowls and serve.

Nutrition
Calories 89, fat 6.8, carbs 6.1, protein 1.7, fiber 2.1

Avocado Tussle with White Mushrooms

Prep Time + Cook time: 30 minutes , Servings: 4

5-Ingredients:
- 1 cup Baby arugula
- ½ cup Veggie stock
- 2 Avocados; pitted and cubed
- ½ lb. Sliced white mushrooms
- 1 tbsp Chopped chives

What you'll need from the store cupboard:
- A pinch of salt and black pepper
- 1 tbsp Balsamic vinegar
- 1 tbsp Olive oil

Directions:
1. Press 'Sauté' on the instant pot and pour in the oil. When hot, add the mushrooms to cook for 4 minutes.
2. Gently pour in the veggie stock, vinegar, salt and pepper, and chives. Stir and seal the lid to cook for 15 minutes at high pressure.
3. Natural release the pressure for 10 minutes. Pour it inside a salad bowl and mix in the baby arugula and the avocado. Serve.

Nutrition
Calories 250, fat 23.3, carbs 7.6, protein 3.8, fiber 6.4

Creamy Salmon with Eggs And Cilantro

Prep Time + Cook time: 22 minutes , Servings: 4

5-Ingredients:
- 4 oz Smoked salmon; skinless and boneless: cut into strips
- 4 Eggs
- 1 tbsp Chopped cilantro
- 1 tbsp Chopped chives
- ½ cup Coconut cream

What you'll need from the store cupboard:
- A pinch of salt and black pepper

- Cooking spray

Directions:
1. Whisk the salmon, cilantro, eggs, chives, cream, salt, and pepper in a bowl.
2. Coat the instant pot with the cooking spray and pour the creamy egg mix into the pot. Seal the lid to cook for 12 minutes on high pressure.
3. Natural release the pressure for 10 minutes, share and serve.

Nutrition
Calories 167, fat 12.9, carbs 2.1, protein 11.4, fiber 0.7

Creamy Walnuts and Cardamom Mousse

Prep Time + Cook time: 15 minutes , Servings: 2

5-Ingredients:
- 1 tsp Ground cardamom
- ½ cup Chopped walnuts
- 1 tsp Swerve
- 2 tbsp Almond meal
- 1 ½ cups Coconut cream

Directions:
1. Combine the cardamom, almond meal, walnuts, cream, and swerve in the instant pot and seal the lid to cook for 10 minutes at high pressure.
2. Quick-release the pressure for 5 minutes, share into bowls and serve.

Nutrition
Calories 231, fat 21.9, carbs 5.1, protein 8.9, fiber 3.2

Her By Mushroom

Prep Time + Cook time: 30 minutes , Servings: 4

5-Ingredients:
- 1 Red bell pepper; cut into strips
- 1 ½ lbs. Chopped brown mushrooms .
- 2 tbsp Chicken stock .

What you'll need from the store cupboard:
- A pinch of salt and black pepper
- 1 tbsp Olive oil
- ½ tsp Garlic powder
- ½ tsp Dried basil
- 1 tsp Chopped rosemary

Directions:
1. Press 'Sauté' on the instant pot and pour in the oil. When it is hot, add the mushrooms and cook for 5 minutes.
2. Mix in the red bell pepper, rosemary, chicken stock, dried basil, garlic powder, salt, and pepper then seal the lid to cook for 15 minutes at high pressure.
3. Natural release the pressure for 10 minutes, share into plates and serve.

Nutrition
Calories 42, fat 3.7, carbs 2.7, protein 0.4, fiber 0.6

Cheesy Chili Eggs

Prep Time + Cook time: 20 minutes , Servings: 4

5-Ingredients:
- 1 cup Shredded cheddar cheese
- 4 Whisked eggs
- 2 tbsp Chopped basil

What you'll need from the store cupboard:
- A pinch of salt and black pepper
- Cooking spray

- 1 tsp Chili powder

Directions:

1. Coat the instant pot with the cooking spray and mix in the basil, chili powder, cheddar cheese, eggs, salt, and pepper then seal the lid to cook for 15 minutes at high pressure.
2. Quick-release the pressure for 5 minutes, share into plates and serve.

Nutrition

Calories 180, fat 14, carbs 1.1, protein 12.7, fiber 0.3

Nutty Blueberries Mix

Prep Time + Cook time: 13 minutes , Servings: 6

5-Ingredients:

- ½ cup Chopped walnuts
- ½ cup Chopped almonds
- 1 cup Blueberries
- 2 tsp Swerve
- 1 cup Coconut cream

What you'll need from the store cupboard:

- 1 tsp Vanilla extract

Directions:

1. Mix all the ingredients in the instant pot and seal the lid to cook for 8 minutes on high pressure.
2. Quick-release the pressure for 5 minutes, share into bowls and serve.

Nutrition

Calories 218, fat 19.7, carbs 5.8, protein 5.3, fiber 3.2

Veggie Pastry

Prep Time + Cook time: 30 minutes , Servings: 4

5-Ingredients:

- 1 tbsp Chopped chives
- ½ cup Chopped kale
- ½ cup Chopped Bok Choy
- ½ cup Almond milk
- 4 Whisked eggs

What you'll need from the store cupboard:

- 1 tbsp Avocado oil
- A pinch of salt and pepper
- 1½ cup of water

Directions:

1. Mix the chives, kale, Bok Choy, almond milk, eggs, salt, and pepper in a bowl.
2. Coat the muffin pastry tray with oil and pour the mix into it.
3. Pour the 1 and 1/2 cup of water into the instant pot, put in the inner pot and place the pastry tray inside it. Seal the lid to cook for 20 minutes at high pressure.
4. Natural release the pressure for 10 minutes and let the pastry cool down and serve.

Nutrition

Calories 142, fat 12, carbs 3.3, protein 6.7, fiber 1.1

Artichoke And Spinach Scones

Prep Time + Cook time: 30 minutes , Servings: 12

5-Ingredients:

- 4 Eggs
- 1 cup Baby spinach; chopped
- 2 cup Canned artichoke hearts; drained and chopped
- 3 cups Almond flour
- 1 tsp Baking soda

What you'll need from the store cupboard:

- A pinch of salt and black pepper
- Cooking spray
- 1 ½ cups water

Directions:

1. Combine the eggs, spinach, baking soda, artichoke hearts, almond flour, salt, and pepper in a bowl and set aside.
2. Coat the muffin tray with cooking spray and pour the spinach mix in the tray.
3. Pour the 1 ½ cups water into the instant pot and place the inner pot inside it. Put the muffin tray inside the pot and seal the lid to cook for 20 minutes at high pressure.
4. Natural release the pressure for 10 minutes and let the scones cool and serve.

Nutrition

Calories 66, fat 4.5, carbs 0.6, protein 5.8, fiber 0.2

Creamy Zucchini

Prep Time + Cook time: 22 minutes , Servings: 4

5-Ingredients:

- 4 Sliced zucchini
- 1 tbsp Chopped dill
- ½ cup Veggie stock
- ½ cup Softened cream cheese
- ½ cup Heavy cream

What you'll need from the store cupboard:

- A pinch of salt and black pepper
- 1 tbsp Avocado oil
- 2 cloves Minced garlic

Directions:

1. Put the zucchini in the instant pot and mix in the stock, salt, and pepper then seal the lid to cook for 12 minutes at high pressure.
2. Natural release the pressure for 10 minutes, strain the zucchini and put it in a food processor. Mix in the rest of the ingredients and blend well. Share into bowls and serve as a spread.

Nutrition

Calories 193, fat 16.5, carbs 7.8, protein 5.2, fiber 2.5

Cheesy Radish And Tomatoes Jumble

Prep Time + Cook time: 20 minutes , Servings: 4

5-Ingredients:

- ¼ cup Sliced radishes
- ½ cup Shredded mozzarella
- 1 tbsp Chopped chives
- 1 lb. Halved cherry tomatoes
- 1 tbsp Chopped basil

What you'll need from the store cupboard:

- A pinch of salt and black pepper
- 1 tbsp Olive oil

Directions:

1. Put the chives, radishes, basil, tomatoes, olive oil, salt, and pepper inside the instant pot and mix it well.
2. Drizzle the mozzarella cheese over the spread and seal the lid to cook for 10 minutes at high pressure.
3. Natural release the pressure for 10 minutes, share into plates and serve.

Nutrition
Calories 62, fat 4.4, carbs 4.9, protein 2.1, fiber 1.5

Nutty Coconut Mousse

Prep Time + Cook time: 10 minutes , Servings: 6
5-Ingredients:
- 2 cups Coconut milk
- 4 tsp Swerve
- ½ cup Unsweetened and shredded coconut
- ¼ cup Chopped walnuts
- 1 cup Coconut cream

Directions:
1. Mix all the ingredients in the instant pot and seal the lid to cook for 5 minutes at high pressure.
2. Quick-release the pressure for 5 minutes, share into bowls and serve.

Nutrition
Calories 332, fat 33.8, carbs 7.8, protein 4.2, fiber 3.6

Garlic Pork Meat With Kale

Prep Time + Cook time: 25 minutes , Servings: 4
5-Ingredients:
- 1 Lb. Torn kale .
- 1 Chopped spring onion
- ½ cup Beef stock
- 2 cups Ground pork meat

What you'll need from the store cupboard:
- A pinch of salt and black pepper
- 1 tbsp Avocado oil .
- 2 cloves Minced garlic

Directions:
1. Press 'Sauté' on the instant pot and pour in the oil. When hot, add the garlic, onion, and pork meat to brown for 5 minutes.
2. Mix in the kale, spring onion, beef stock, salt, and pepper and seal the lid to cook for 10 minutes on high pressure.
3. Natural release the pressure for 10 minutes, share into plates and serve.

Nutrition
Calories 66, fat 5.3, carbs 6.5, protein 3.8, fiber 2

Creamy Zucchini With Walnuts

Prep Time + Cook time: 20 minutes , Servings: 4
5-Ingredients:
- ¼ cup Chopped walnuts
- 2 tbsp Swerve
- 1 tsp Ground nutmeg
- 4 Sliced zucchinis
- 1 ½ cups Coconut cream

Directions:
1. Mix all the ingredients in the instant pot and seal the lid to cook for 10 minutes on high pressure.

2. Natural release the pressure for 10 minutes, share into bowls and serve.

Nutrition
Calories 83, fat 8.2, carbs 7.8, protein 4.3, fiber 2.8

Bacon And Turkey Frittata With Avocado And Tomatoes

Prep Time + Cook time: 25 minutes , Servings: 4
5-Ingredients:
- 2 Bacon slices: cooked and crumbled
- 1 cup Skinless and boneless turkey breast; cut into strips
- 1 Chopped tomato
- 1 Small avocado; peeled and chopped
- 4 Whisked eggs

What you'll need from the store cupboard:
- A pinch of salt and black pepper
- 2 tbsp Olive oil

Directions:

1. Press 'Sauté' on the instant pot and add 1 tablespoon of olive oil to the pot. When hot, add the turkey to brown for 5 minutes.
2. Mix in the remaining ingredients and seal the lid to cook for 10 minutes at high pressure.
3. Natural release the pressure for 10 minutes, share the frittata and serve.

Nutrition
Calories 228, fat 21.2, carbs 5.3, protein 6.6, fiber 3.6

Creamy Nuts And Strawberries

Prep Time + Cook time: 20 minutes , Servings: 4
5-Ingredients:
- ½ cup Chopped almonds
- ½ tsp Ground nutmeg
- 2 cups Strawberries; halved
- ½ cup Chopped walnuts
- 1 cup Coconut cream

What you'll need from the store cupboard:
- 1 tbsp Stevia

Directions:

1. Mix the cream, almonds, nutmeg, strawberries, walnuts, and stevia in the instant pot and seal the lid to cook for 10 minutes on low pressure.
2. Natural release the pressure for 10 minutes, share into bowls and serve.

Nutrition
Calories 328, fat 29.8, carbs 7.6, protein 8.1, fiber 5.4

Garlic Turkey With Leeks And Egg

Prep Time + Cook time: 25 minutes , Servings: 4
5-Ingredients:
- 1 Skinless and boneless turkey breasts; cut into strips
- 2 Chopped leeks
- 8 Whisked eggs
- ½ cup Chicken stock

What you'll need from the store cupboard:
- 2 tbsp Olive oil .
- 2 cloves Minced garlic

Directions:
1. Press 'Sauté' on the instant pot and add the oil. When it is hot, mix in the turkey, garlic, and leeks to cook for 5 minutes.

2. Mix in the eggs and chicken stock then seal the lid to cook on high pressure for 10 minutes.
3. Natural release the pressure for 10 minutes, share into plates and serve.

Nutrition
Calories 216, fat 16, carbs 7.6, protein 11.9, fiber 0.8

Coconut and Berries Mix

Prep Time + Cook time: 22 minutes , Servings: 6

5-Ingredients:
- 1 tsp Swerve
- 3 tbsp Unsweetened coconut flakes
- 2 cups Almond milk
- 1 cup Blackberries
- 1 cup Strawberries

What you'll need from the store cupboard:
- 1 tsp Vanilla extract

Directions:

1. Combine all the ingredients in the instant pot and seal the lid to cook for 12 minutes at high pressure.
2. Natural release the pressure for 10 minutes, share into bowls and serve.

Nutrition
Calories 213, fat 20.1, carbs 6.7, protein 2.4, fiber 3.7

Chili Mushrooms with Okra Egg Dish

Prep Time + Cook time: 25 minutes , Servings: 2

5-Ingredients:
- 4 Whisked eggs
- ½ cup Chopped cilantro
- 1 lb. Sliced white mushrooms
- 1 cup Okra
- 2 Chopped spring onions

What you'll need from the store cupboard:
- 1 tbsp Avocado oil
- 2 Minced garlic cloves
- 2 Minced chili peppers

Directions:
1. Press 'Sauté' on the instant pot and add the oil. When hot, mix in the garlic and onions to reduce for 2 minutes.

2. Add in the mushrooms to cook for 2 minutes.
3. Mix the eggs, cilantro, okra, and chili peppers with the mushrooms in the pot and seal the lid to cook for 10 minutes at high pressure.
4. Natural release the pressure for 10 minutes, share the egg dish and serve.

Nutrition
Calories 108, fat 5.2, carbs 4.7, protein 9.9, fiber 2.4

Creamy Cocoa Vanilla Coconut Meal

Prep Time + Cook time: 20 minutes , Servings: 6

5-Ingredients:
- 1 cup Almond milk
- 1 cup Unsweetened coconut flakes
- 1 tsp Cocoa powder
- 1 cup Coconut cream

What you'll need from the store cupboard:

- 2 tsp Vanilla extract
- 2 tbsp Stevia

Directions:
1. Combine all the ingredients in the instant pot and seal the lid to cook for 10 minutes at high pressure.

2. Natural release the pressure for 10 minutes then share into bowls and serve.
Nutrition

Calories 236, fat 23.6, carbs 6.5, protein 2.3, fiber 3.1

Creamy Almonds And Broccoli With Coconut

Prep Time + Cook time: 20 minutes , Servings: 4

5-Ingredients:
- 1 cup Broccoli florets
- 2 Whisked eggs
- ½ cup Coconut flakes
- ½ cup Toasted and chopped almonds
- 1 cup Heavy cream

What you'll need from the store cupboard:
- Cooking spray

Directions:
1. Coat the instant pot with the cooking spray and mix in the almonds and the broccoli florets then pour in the heavy cream mixed with the eggs over the broccoli and nuts.
2. Drizzle the coconut flakes over the mix then seal the lid to cook for 15 minutes at high pressure.
3. Natural release the pressure for 10 minutes, share into plates and serve.

Nutrition
Calories 248, fat 22.8, carbs 6.6, protein 6.9, fiber 3

Creamy Coconut Frittata

Prep Time + Cook time: 20 minutes , Servings: 4

5-Ingredients:
- 4 Whisked eggs
- ½ cup Coconut milk
- 1 cup Coconut flakes

What you'll need from the store cupboard:
- A pinch of salt and black pepper
- Cooking spray
- 1 tbsp Sweet paprika

Directions:
1. Whisk the paprika, eggs, coconut milk, salt, pepper, and coconut flakes in a bowl.
2. Spray the instant pot with the cooking spray and pour in the egg mix then seal the lid to cook for 10 minutes at high pressure.
3. Natural release the pressure for 10 minutes, share the frittata and serve.

Nutrition
Calories 209, fat 18.6, carbs 6, protein 7.2, fiber 3.1

Eggs and Tomatoes with Avocado

Prep Time + Cook time: 8 minutes , Servings: 2

5-Ingredients:
- 4 eggs
- 1 avocado; peeled and cubed
- 1 tomato; cubed
- 2 cups water

What you'll need from the store cupboard:
- 1 tsp balsamic vinegar
- A pinch of salt and black pepper
- 2 tsp avocado oil

Directions:
1. Pour some water into the instant pot and place the steaming basket inside the pot then put the eggs inside the basket and seal the lid to cook for 3 minutes on low pressure.

2. Quick-release the pressure for 5 minutes, then let the eggs cool, then peel and cut into quarters and put in a bowl.
3. Mix in the tomatoes, avocado, vinegar, oil, salt and pepper and flip to coat.

4. Serve into bowls.

Nutrition

Calories 170, fat 14.7, carbs 5.5, protein 6, fiber 3.2

Creamy Cinnamon And Coconut With Strawberries

Prep Time + Cook time: 15 minutes , Servings: 6

5-Ingredients:
- 1 cup Halved strawberries
- 2 cups Almond milk
- 1 cup Coconut flakes
- 1 tbsp Cinnamon powder
- ½ cup Coconut cream

Directions:

1. Mix all the ingredients together in the instant pot and seal the lid to cook for 10 minutes at high pressure.
2. Quick-release the pressure for 5 minutes, share into bowls and serve.

Nutrition

Calories 285, fat 28.4, carbs 7.5, protein 2.9, fiber 3.9

Spicy Leek And Veggie Egg Dish

Prep Time + Cook time: 25 minutes , Servings: 4

5-Ingredients:
- 1 Chopped red bell pepper
- 4 Whisked eggs
- 2 Sliced leeks
- 1 Chopped shallot

What you'll need from the store cupboard:
- A pinch of salt and black pepper
- Cooking spray
- 1 tbsp Sweet paprika .

Directions:

1. Coat the instant pot with the cooking spray then mix in all the ingredients and seal the lid to cook for 15 minutes at high pressure.
2. Natural release the pressure for 10 minutes, share into bowls and serve.

Nutrition

Calories 106, fat 9.4, carbs 6.6, protein 6.8, fiber 1.9

Cauliflower Rice With Broccoli And Tomatoes

Prep Time + Cook time: 22 minutes , Servings: 6

5-Ingredients:
- 1 tsp Chili flakes
- 1 Broccoli head with florets separated
- 4 Cubed tomatoes
- 1 cup Veggie stock
- 1 cup Cauliflower rice

What you'll need from the store cupboard:
- 2 tsp Curry powder
- 1 tbsp Grated ginger

Directions:

1. Mix all the ingredients in the instant pot and seal the lid to cook at high pressure for 12 minutes.
2. Natural release the pressure for 10 minutes, share into bowls and serve.

Nutrition

Calories 30, fat 5, carbs 4.5, protein 1.3, fiber 1.3

Chapter 4 Fish and Seafood Recipes

Easy Lemon Pepper Salmon

Prep Time + Cook time:8 minutes , Servings: 4

Ingredients:

- 3 sprigs fresh herbs (your choice)
- 1 pound boneless salmon fillets
- ½ lemon, sliced thin
- ¾ cup of water

What you'll need from the store cupboard:

- Salt and pepper
- 1 tablespoon olive oil

Directions:

1. Pour ¾ cup of water in the Instant Pot and add the herbs.
2. Place the steamer rack in the pot and place the salmon on it, skin-side-down.
3. Season with salt and pepper then drizzle with oil and layer with lemon slices.
4. Close and lock the lid.
5. Press the Steam button and adjust the timer to 3 minutes.
6. When the timer goes off, do a Quick Release by pressing Cancel and switching the steam valve to "venting."
7. When the pot has depressurized, open the lid.
8. Remove the salmon to a plate and serve immediately.

Nutrition:

calories 180 fat 10.5g ,protein 22g ,carbs 0g ,fiber 0g ,net carbs 0g

Shrimp Bisque

Prep Time + Cook time:9 minutes , Servings: 8

Ingredients:

- 1 small yellow onion, chopped
- 2 (14-ounce) cans diced tomatoes
- 4 cups chicken broth
- 1 tablespoon Old Bay seasoning
- 24 ounces fresh shrimp tails

What you'll need from the store cupboard:

- 2 cups heavy cream
- 2 tablespoons butter
- Salt and pepper to taste

Directions:

1. Turn the Instant Pot on to the Sauté setting and let it heat up.
2. Add the butter and let it melt then sauté the onions for 3 minutes.
3. Stir in the diced tomatoes, chicken broth, and Old Bay seasoning.
4. Add the shrimp tails and season with salt and pepper.
5. Close and lock the lid, then press the Manual button and adjust the timer to 4 minutes.
6. When the timer goes off, let the pressure vent naturally.
7. When the pot has depressurized, open the lid.
8. Remove the shrimp tails and separate the meat. Chop it coarsely then add it back to the pot.
9. Stir in the cream, then adjust seasoning to taste and serve hot.

Nutrition:

calories 245 fat 15.5g ,protein 20g ,carbs 6g ,fiber 1.5g ,net carbs 4.5g

Shrimp Scampi

Prep Time + Cook time:6 minutes , Servings: 6

Ingredients:
- ½ cup chicken broth
- 2 pounds large shrimp, peeled and deveined

What you'll need from the store cupboard:
- Salt and pepper
- 3 cloves minced garlic
- ¼ cup butter
- 1 tablespoon fresh lemon juice
- ½ cup dry white wine

Directions:
1. Turn the Instant Pot on to the Sauté setting and let it heat up.
2. Add the butter and garlic, then cook for 1 minute, stirring.
3. Pour in the wine and cook for a minute or two before adding the chicken broth.
4. Add the shrimp then close and lock the lid.
5. Press the Meat/Stew button and adjust the timer to 1 minute.
6. When the timer goes off, let the pressure vent for 5 minutes then do a Quick Release by pressing Cancel and switching the steam valve to "venting."
7. When the pot has depressurized, open the lid.
8. Stir in the lemon juice then season with salt and pepper and serve hot.

Nutrition:
calories 215 fat 8g ,protein 29g ,carbs 4g ,fiber 0g ,net carbs 4g

Coconut Fish Curry

Prep Time + Cook time:15 minutes , Servings: 6

Ingredients:
- 1 tablespoon coconut oil
- 1 small yellow onion, diced
- 2 cups unsweetened coconut milk
- 1 medium tomato, diced
- 1 ½ pounds white fish fillet, cut into 2-inch pieces

What you'll need from the store cupboard:
- 1 tablespoon fresh grated ginger
- 1 tablespoon curry powder
- Salt and pepper to taste

Directions:
1. Press the Sauté button on the Instant Pot and let it heat up.
2. Add the oil then stir in the onion and ginger – cook for 2 minutes.
3. Stir in the coconut milk and curry powder then cook for 1 minute more.
4. Add the diced tomatoes and fish, stirring to coat, then close and lock the lid.
5. Press the Manual button and adjust the timer to 5 minutes on Low Pressure.
6. When the timer goes off, do a Quick Release by pressing Cancel and switching the steam valve to "venting."
7. When the pot has depressurized, open the lid.
8. Adjust the seasoning to taste then serve hot.

Nutrition:
calories 245 fat 12.5g ,protein 28g ,carbs 4g ,fiber 1.5g ,net carbs 2.5g

Ginger Soy Salmon

Prep Time + Cook time:8 minutes , Servings: 4

Ingredients:

- 1 pound boneless salmon fillet

What you'll need from the store cupboard:

- Salt and pepper
- 2 cloves minced garlic
- 1 tablespoon fresh grated ginger
- 2 tablespoons soy sauce
- 2 tablespoons fresh lime juice
- 2 cups of water

Directions:

1. Place the steamer rack in the Instant Pot and add 2 cups of water.
2. Whisk together the lime juice, soy sauce, ginger, and garlic in a large zippered freezer bag.
3. Season the salmon with salt and pepper then add to the bag.
4. Shake to coat then marinate for 30 minutes. Place the bag in the Instant Pot on top of the steamer rack then close and lock the lid.
5. Press the Manual button and adjust the timer to 3 minutes on Low Pressure.
6. When the timer goes off, let the pressure vent for 5 minutes then do a Quick Release by pressing Cancel and switching the steam valve to "venting."
7. When the pot has depressurized, open the lid.
8. Transfer the salmon to a roasting pan and broil for 3 minutes. Serve hot.

Nutrition:

calories 165 fat 7g ,protein 23g ,carbs 3g ,fiber 0.5g ,net carbs 2.5g

Steamed Mussels

Prep Time + Cook time:10 minutes , Servings: 4

Ingredients:

- 2 pounds live mussels
- 1 small yellow onion, chopped
- ¾ cup chicken broth

What you'll need from the store cupboard:

- 2 cloves minced garlic
- 2 tablespoons butter
- ¼ cup white wine

Directions:

1. Rinse the mussels well and clean them, discarding any that are open.
2. Turn the Instant Pot on to the Sauté function and let it heat up.
3. Melt the butter then add the onions and garlic, cooking for 3 minutes.
4. Stir in the chicken broth and wine, then scrape up any browned bits.
5. Add the mussels then close and lock the lid.
6. Press the Manual button and adjust the timer to 5 minutes.
7. When the timer goes off, let the pressure vent naturally.
8. When the pot has depressurized, open the lid.
9. Spoon the mussels into bowls using a slotted spoon and serve with melted butter.

Nutrition:

calories 280 fat 11g ,protein 28g ,carbs 11.5g ,fiber 0.5g ,net carbs 10g

Lemon Tilapia Packets

Prep Time + Cook time:13 minutes , Servings: 4

Ingredients:

- 4 (6-ounce) tilapia fillets, boneless
- ½ teaspoon paprika
- 4 slices lemon
- 1 ½ cups of water

What you'll need from the store cupboard:

- Salt and pepper
- 2 tablespoons olive oil

Directions:

1. Place the steamer rack in the Instant Pot and add 1 ½ cups of water.
2. Cut out four pieces of parchment paper and place a tilapia fillet on each.
3. Brush the fillets with oil then season with paprika, salt, and pepper.
4. Top each fillet with a slice of lemon then fold the parchment paper into packets.
5. Place the packets on the steamer insert, then close and lock the lid.
6. Press the Manual button and adjust the timer to 8 minutes.
7. When the timer goes off, do a Quick Release by pressing Cancel and switching the steam valve to "venting."
8. When the pot has depressurized, open the lid.
9. Remove the packets and serve the fish immediately.

Nutrition:
calories 250 fat 13g ,protein 31g ,carbs 1g ,fiber 1g ,net carbs 1g

Steamed Crab Legs

Prep Time + Cook time:8 minutes , Servings: 4

Ingredients:

- 2 pounds crab legs
- 1 cup of water

What you'll need from the store cupboard:

- ½ cup butter, melted

Directions:

1. Place the steamer rack in the Instant Pot and add 1 cup of water.
2. Add the crab legs to the pot, then close and lock the lid.
3. Press the Manual button and adjust the timer to 3 minutes.
4. When the timer goes off, do a Quick Release by pressing Cancel and switching the steam valve to "venting."
5. When the pot has depressurized, open the lid.
6. Remove the crab legs to a platter using tongs and serve with melted butter.

Nutrition:
calories 315 fat 25g ,protein 21.5g ,carbs 0g ,fiber 0g ,net carbs 0g

Coconut Shrimp

Prep Time + Cook time:15 minutes , Servings: 4

Ingredients:

- 1 pound large shrimp, peeled and deveined
- ¾ cup canned coconut milk
- 1 teaspoon turmeric
- Pinch cayenne
- 2 cups of water

What you'll need from the store cupboard:

- 1 tablespoon minced garlic

- 1 tablespoon fresh grated ginger

Directions:

1. Place the steamer rack in the Instant Pot and add 2 cups of water.
2. Whisk together the coconut milk, ginger, garlic, turmeric, and cayenne in a bowl.
3. Toss in the shrimp then transfer to a heatproof bowl and cover with foil.
4. Place the bowl in the Instant Pot on top of the trivet, then close and lock the lid.
5. Press the Manual button and adjust the timer to 4 minutes on Low Pressure.
6. When the timer goes off, do a Quick Release by pressing Cancel and switching the steam valve to "venting."
7. When the pot has depressurized, open the lid and remove the bowl to serve.

Nutrition:

calories 205 fat 11g ,protein 22.5g ,carbs 6.5g ,fiber 1.5g ,net carbs 5g

Chili Lime Salmon

Prep Time + Cook time:10 minutes , Servings: 4

Ingredients:

- 4 (6-ounce) boneless salmon fillets
- 2 limes, juiced
- 2 jalapenos, seeded and minced
- 1 teaspoon paprika
- 1 cup of water

What you'll need from the store cupboard:

- Salt and pepper
- 2 tablespoons olive oil
- 2 cloves minced garlic

Directions:

1. Place the steamer rack in the Instant Pot and add 1 cup of water.
2. Season the salmon with salt and pepper then place it on the steamer rack.
3. Close and lock the lid then press the Steam button and adjust the timer to 5 minutes.
4. When the timer goes off, do a Quick Release by pressing Cancel and switching the steam valve to "venting."
5. When the pot has depressurized, open the lid.
6. Whisk together the lime juice, olive oil, jalapeno, garlic, and paprika in a bowl.
7. Remove the salmon from the pot and drizzle with the glaze to serve.

Nutrition:

calories 295 fat 17.5g ,protein 33.5g ,carbs 3g ,fiber 0.5g ,net carbs 2.5g

Spicy Cod with Cilantro

Prep Time + Cook time: 17 minutes , Servings: 4

5-Ingredients:

- 1 tbsp Chopped cilantro
- 1 lb Cod fillets; boneless, skinless and cubed
- 1 cup Chicken stock
- 1 tbsp Hot sauce
- 1 tbsp Hot paprika

What you'll need from the store cupboard:

- A pinch of salt and black pepper

Directions:

1. Mix all the ingredients in the instant pot and seal the lid to cook for 12 minutes at high pressure.
2. Quick-release the pressure for 5 minutes, ladle into bowls and serve.

Nutrition

Calories 100, fat 4.3, carbs 3.2, protein 1.4, fiber 1

Sweet Chive Fillet

Prep Time + Cook time: 17 minutes , Servings: 4

5-Ingredients:
- 4 pieces Trout fillets
- half cup Chicken stock
- 1 tablespoon Chives (crushed)
- 2 teaspoons Sweet paprika
- half teaspoon Oregano

What you'll need from the store cupboard:
- Salt and Black pepper to taste

Directions:

1. In the instant pot, mix the trout with the other ingredients, cover it and heat on high temperature for 11 minutes.
2. Release the pressure rapidly for 4 minutes, split them among plates before eating.

Nutritional Info per Servings:
Calories: 132, Fat: 5.5g, Fiber: 0.5g, Carbs: 0.9g, Protein: 16.8g

Salty Cilantro Shrimp

Prep Time + Cook time: 13 minutes , Servings: 4

5-Ingredients:
- 1 lb Shrimp
- 1 piece Lime zest
- 1 cup Chicken stock
- ¼ cup Cilantro (sliced)
- 1 piece Lime juice

What you'll need from the store cupboard:
- Salt and Black pepper to taste

Directions:

1. In the instant pot, mix the shrimp with the other ingredients then place the cover on and heat on high temperature for 8 minutes.
2. Release the pressure quickly for 5 minutes, split the shrimp among plates and eat with sides.

Nutritional Info per Servings:
Calories: 138, Fat: 3.8g, Fiber: 0g, Carbs: 2g, Protein: 26g

Shrimp and Leeks Appetizer

Prep time + Cook time: 10 minutes , Servings: 6

5-Ingredients:
- 2 lbs. (peeled and deveined) Shrimp
- 2 (sliced) Leeks
- 1 tbsp (chopped) Chives
- 2 (minced) Garlic cloves
- ½ cup Veggie stock

What you'll need from the store cupboard:
- 1 tbsp Olive oil
- 1 tbsp Sweet paprika

Directions:

1. Let your Instant Pot preheat on Sauté mode.
2. Add oil, leeks, and garlic, then sauté for 1 minute.
3. Stir in remaining ingredients except for chives and mix well.
4. Seal the pot's lid and cook for 4 minutes on manual mode at High.
5. Allow the pressure to release in 5 minutes naturally then remove the lid.
6. Garnish with chives.
7. Serve fresh and enjoy.

Nutrition:
Calories 224, Total Fat: 5.1g, Carbs: 3.9g, Protein: 35.1g, Fiber: 1g.

Tomato Trout Dish

Prep Time + Cook time: 17 minutes , Servings: 4

5-Ingredients:

- 4 pieces Trout fillets
- 1 tbsp Parsley (sliced)
- 2 cups Red radishes
- 2 tbsp Tomato passata

What you'll need from the store cupboard:

- Salt and Black pepper to taste

Directions:

1. In the instant pot, put all the ingredients then cover it and heat on elevated temperature for 12 minutes.
2. Release the pressure quickly for 5 minutes, split entirely among plates before eating.

Nutritional Info per Servings:

Calories: 129, Fat: 5.3g, Fiber: 1.1g, Carbs: 2.5g, Protein: 17g

Cod broccoli fillet

Prep Time + Cook time: 20 minutes , Servings: 4

5-Ingredients:

- 4 pieces Cod fillets
- 1 lb. Broccoli florets
- 1 tbsp Cilantro
- 1 cup Chicken stock
- 2 tbsp Tomato passata

What you'll need from the store cupboard:

- Salt and Black pepper to taste

Directions:

1. In the instant pot mix all the ingredients, cover it and cook on elevated temperatures for approximately 15 minutes.
2. Release the pressure quickly for 5 minutes, split them among plates before eating.

Nutritional Info per Servings:

Calories: 197, Fat: 5.3g, Fiber: 3.1g, Carbs: 4.3g, Protein: 19.4g

Rosemary Cloves Trout Fillet

Prep Time + Cook time: 25 minutes , Servings: 4

5-Ingredients:

- 4 pieces (no bones and skin) Trout fillets
- 2 cups Cauliflower florets
- half cup Veggie stock
- 2 pieces Garlic cloves
- 1 tbsp Rosemary (sliced)

What you'll need from the store cupboard:

- 1 tbsp Avocado oil
- Salt and Black pepper to taste

Directions:

1. Put the instant pot on Sauté option then put the oil, cook it then place the garlic and cook for 120 seconds.
2. Put all of the other ingredients cover it and heat it on elevated temperature for 13 minutes.
3. Remove the pressure gradually for 10 minutes, split them among plates before eating.

Nutritional Info per Servings:

Calories: 140, Fat: 5.9g, Fiber: 1.8g, Carbs: 3.9g, Protein: 17.7g

Spicy Turmeric Cod Fillet

Prep Time + Cook time: 17 minutes , Servings: 4

5-Ingredients:
- 4 pieces (no bones and skin) Cod fillets
- 1 teaspoon Turmeric powder
- 1 tbsp Chili paste
- 3 pieces Garlic cloves (crushed)
- 1 cup Tomato passata

Directions:
1. In the instant pot, mix the cod with the other ingredients and cover it then cook on elevated temperature for about 12 minutes.
2. Release the pressure quickly for 5 minutes then split them among plates before eating.

Nutritional Info per Servings:
Calories: 244, Fat: 12, Fiber: 1.6g, Carbs: 4.5g, Protein: 14.6g

Veggie Mackerel Basil Mix

Prep Time + Cook time: 25 minutes , Servings: 4

5-Ingredients:
- 1 lb. Mackerel
- 2 pieces Chili peppers (sliced)
- 1 cup Veggie stock
- half cup Basil (sliced)

What you'll need from the store cupboard:
- Salt and Black pepper to taste
- 2 tbsp Olive oil
- 2 tsp Red pepper flakes

Directions:
1. Put the instant pot to Sauté mode, put the oil and cook it then put the pepper flakes and chili pepper then heat it for 120 seconds.
2. Put the other ingredients, then cover it and cook for 12 minutes under high temperature.
3. Release the pressure gradually for 10 minutes and split all of them among plates before eating.

Nutritional Info per Servings:
Calories: 362, Fat: 14.7, Fiber: 4.1g, Carbs: 0.8g, Protein: 27.5g

Vegan Tomato Tuna

Prep Time + Cook time: 22 minutes , Servings: 4

5-Ingredients:
- 14 oz Tomatoes (sliced)
- 1 piece Shallot (sliced)
- 1 cup Black olives
- 1 lb. (no skin and bones) Tuna (squared)
- 2 tbsp Oregano (sliced)

What you'll need from the store cupboard:
- 2 tbsp Avocado oil

Directions:
1. Put the instant pot on Sauté mode, then put the oil and cook it. Also, put the shallot and cook it for another 120 seconds.
2. Put the tuna and the other ingredients and cover it then heat it on high temperature for another 9 or 10 minutes.
3. Release the pressure gradually for 10 minutes then split them among plates before eating.

Nutritional Info per Servings:
Calories: 284, Fat: 14.1, Fiber: 3.5g, Carbs: 6.7g, Protein: 31.4g

Glazed Salmon

Prep Time + Cook time: 25 minutes , Servings: 4

5-Ingredients:

- 4 pieces Boneless salmon fillets
- 3 tbsp Swerve
- 1 tbsp Coconut amino

What you'll need from the store cupboard:

- 1 tsp Balsamic vinegar
- Salt and Black pepper to taste
- 4 tsp Mustard

Directions:

1. Put the instant pot on Sauté option, then put the mustard, swerve, vinegar, seasoning and amino excluding the fish, cook it then whips it and heats for 3 minutes.
2. Put the salmon then cover it and heat for another 12 minutes on high temperature.
3. Release the pressure gradually for 10 minutes, then split the salmon among your plates then put the glaze above it before eating.

Nutritional Info per Servings:

Calories: 251, Fat: 11.9, Fiber: 0.5g, Carbs: 1.2g, Protein: 35.4g

Spicy Tilapia and Kale

Prep Time + Cook time: 30 minutes , Servings: 4

5-Ingredients:

- 4 pcs Boneless tilapia fillets
- 1 bunch Kale (sliced)
- 14 oz. Canned tomatoes (pounded)
- 1 tsp Fennel seed
- 2 pcs. Garlic cloves (sliced)

What you'll need from the store cupboard:

- Salt and Black pepper to taste
- 3 tbsp Olive oil
- half tsp Pepper flakes (red)

Directions:

1. Put the instant pot on Sauté option, then put the oil, cook it then put the fennel seed and garlic and heat for 3 minutes.
2. Put the other ingredients excluding the fish, and stir then cook for about 4 minutes.
3. Put the tilapia then cover it and heat for another 12 minutes on high temperature.
4. Release the pressure gradually for 10 minutes, then split them among your plates then put the glaze above it before eating.

Nutritional Info per Servings:

Calories: 138, Fat: 11.2, Fiber: 1.5g, Carbs: 4.8g, Protein: 6.3g

Cod Fillets in Cilantro Lime

Prep Time + Cook time: 25 minutes , Servings: 4

5-Ingredients:
- 4 pieces Boneless Cod fillets
- 2 tsp Lime zest
- 3 tbsp Cilantro (sliced)
- half cup Chicken stock
- 2 tbsp Lime juice

What you'll need from the store cupboard:
- Salt and Black pepper to taste
- 1 tbsp Olive oil
- half teaspoon Cumin

Directions:
1. Put the instant pot on Sauté option, then put the oil and heat it. After that, put the cod and cook it for 60 seconds on each portion.
2. Put the other ingredients then cover it and heat for another 13 minutes on high temperature.
3. Release the pressure gradually for 10 minutes then split them among your plates before eating.

Nutritional Info per Servings:
Calories: 187, Fat: 13.1, Fiber: 0.2g, Carbs: 1.6g, Protein: 16.1g

Cajun Shrimp and Salmon Fillet Blend

Prep Time + Cook time: 25 minutes , Servings: 4

5-Ingredients:
- 4 pieces Boneless salmon fillets
- half cup Chicken stock
- 1 lb. Shrimp
- 1 piece Lemon juice
- 2 tbsp Tomato passata

What you'll need from the store cupboard:
- Salt and Black pepper to taste
- 2 tbsp Olive oil
- 1 tsp Cajun seasoning

Directions:
1. Put the instant pot on Sauté option, then put the oil and heat it. After that, put the whole ingredients excluding the shrimp and salmon then cook it for 180 seconds.
2. Put the salmon and heat it for 120 seconds on each side.
3. Put the shrimp then cover it and heat for another 10 minutes on high temperature.
4. Release the pressure gradually for 5 minutes then split them among your plates before eating.

Nutritional Info per Servings:
Calories: 393, Fat: 20, Fiber: 0.1g, Carbs: 2.2g, Protein: 25g

Salty and Sour Parsley Shrimp Dish

Prep Time + Cook time: 13 minutes , Servings: 4

5-Ingredients:

- 2 lbs. Shrimp
- 1 tbsp Parsley (sliced)
- half cup Chicken stock
- 1 tsp Turmeric powder

What you'll need from the store cupboard:

- 1 tbsp Avocado oil
- Salt and Black pepper to taste

Directions:

1. Put the instant pot on Sauté option, then put the oil and heat it. After that, put the whole ingredients for 8 minutes on a high temperature.
2. Release the pressure gradually for 5 minutes then split them among your plates before eating.

Nutritional Info per Servings:

Calories: 278, Fat: 4.4, Fiber: 0.3g, Carbs: 3.4g, Protein: 27.5g

Veggie Tomato Cod Fillet

Prep Time + Cook time: 22 minutes , Servings: 4

5-Ingredients:

- 1 lb. Skinless cod fillet
- half cup Veggie stock
- 10 oz Canned tomatoes (sliced)
- 2 pieces Garlic cloves
- 2 tbsp Basil (crushed)

What you'll need from the store cupboard:

- 2 tbsp Avocado oil

Directions:

1. Put the instant pot on Sauté option, then put the oil and heat it then put the garlic and stir it for 120 seconds.
2. After that, put the whole ingredients for 10 minutes on a high temperature.
3. Release the pressure gradually for 10 minutes then split them among your containers before eating.

Nutritional Info per Servings:

Calories: 240, Fat: 10.7, Fiber: 1.2g, Carbs: 3.7g, Protein: 31.1g

Tomato Garlic Salmon Fillet with Spinach

Prep Time + Cook time: 25 minutes , Servings: 4

5-Ingredients:

- 1 and a half lbs. Boneless salmon fillets
- 1 tbsp Sage
- 1 lb. Small spinaches
- 3 pieces Garlic cloves
- 1 cup Tomato passata

What you'll need from the store cupboard:

- 2 tbsp Avocado oil
- Salt and Black pepper to taste

Directions:

1. Put the instant pot on Sauté option, then put the oil then cook it afterward, put the other ingredients excluding the fish and spinach, swirl it and heat it for 5 minutes.
2. Put the fish and spinach, then cover it and heat it for 10 minutes on high temperature.
3. Release the pressure gradually for 10 minutes then split them among your containers before eating.

Nutritional Info per Servings:

Calories: 355, Fat: 15.4, Fiber: 3.6g, Carbs: 4.6g, Protein: 26.5g

Leafy Crab in Olives Dish

Prep Time + Cook time: 20 minutes , Servings: 4

5-Ingredients:
- 1 tbsp Chives (sliced)
- 1 cup Chicken stock
- 1 cup Baby spinach
- 1 lb. Crab meat
- ¼ cup Tomato passata

What you'll need from the store cupboard:
- 1 tbsp Olive oil

Directions:

1. In the instant pot, mix all the ingredients then cover it up and cook for 10 minutes on high temperature.
2. Release the pressure gradually for 10 minutes then split it among the plates before eating.

Nutritional Info per Servings:
Calories: 138, Fat: 5.7, Fiber: 0.4g, Carbs: 4.3g, Protein: 14.3g

Sweet Bean Tuna Dish

Prep Time + Cook time:22 minutes , Servings: 4

5-Ingredients:
- 1 lb. Green beans
- half tsp Sweet paprika
- 1 tsp Oregano
- 1 and a half cups Tomato passata
- 1 lb. Canned tuna

What you'll need from the store cupboard:
- Salt and Black pepper to taste
- 1 tbsp Olive oil

Directions:

1. Put the instant pot on Sauté option, then put the oil, cook it. Afterward, put the green beans and other ingredients excluding the tuna, then mix and heat it for 5 minutes.
2. Put the fish then cover it and heat it for 7 minutes on high temperature.
3. Release the pressure gradually for 10 minutes, then split them among your containers and put some chives on top of it before eating.

Nutritional Info per Servings:
Calories: 278, Fat: 12.7, Fiber: 3.6g, Carbs: 4.5g, Protein: 27.5g

Halibut Fillet in Tomatoes and Garlic

Prep Time + Cook time: 27 minutes , Servings: 4

5-Ingredients:
- 4 pieces Boneless halibut fillets
- 1 tbsp Parsley
- 1 lb. Brussels sprouts
- 2 pieces Garlic gloves
- 1 cup Tomato passata

What you'll need from the store cupboard:
- 1 tbsp Avocado oil
- Salt and Black pepper to taste

Directions:

1. Put the instant pot on Sauté option, then put the oil and cook it. After that, put the garlic and heat it for 2 minutes.
2. Put the other ingredients and heat it for 10 minutes at high temperature.
3. Release the pressure gradually for 5 minutes, then split them among your containers and put some parsley on top of it before eating.

Nutritional Info per Servings:
Calories: 389, Fat: 7.7g, Fiber: 5.4g, Carbs: 6.1g, Protein: 18.7g

Chapter 5 Poultry Recipes

Indian Butter Chicken

Prep Time + Cook time:20 minutes , Servings: 4

Ingredients:

- 1 small yellow onion, chopped
- 1 pound boneless chicken thighs, chopped
- 1 (14-ounce) can diced tomatoes
- 1 ½ teaspoons ground coriander
- 1 teaspoon ground turmeric

What you'll need from the store cupboard:

- 1 tablespoon olive oil
- ½ cup heavy cream

Directions:

1. Turn the Instant Pot on to the Sauté setting and let it heat up.
2. Add the olive oil then cook the onions until browned.
3. Stir in the chicken, diced tomatoes, and seasonings.
4. Close and lock the lid, then press the Manual button and adjust the timer to 10 minutes.
5. When the timer goes off, let the pressure vent for 10 minutes then do a Quick Release by pressing Cancel and switching the steam valve to "venting."
6. When the pot has depressurized, open the lid.
7. Use a slotted spoon to remove the chicken, the puree and the sauce in the pot.
8. Stir in the heavy cream and the cooked chicken. Serve hot.

Nutrition:

calories 350 fat 26g ,protein 21.5g ,carbs 6g ,fiber 1.5g ,net carbs 4.5g

Turkey-Stuffed Peppers

Prep Time + Cook time:25 , Servings: 4

Ingredients:

- 4 small red bell peppers
- 1 pound ground turkey (85% lean)
- ½ small yellow onion, diced
- ¼ cup grated parmesan cheese
- 1 large egg

What you'll need from the store cupboard:

- Salt and pepper
- ½ cup low-carb tomato sauce
- ½ cup water

Directions:

1. Slice the tops off the peppers and remove the pith.
2. Stir together the ground turkey, onion, and parmesan cheese in a bowl.
3. Add the tomato sauce and egg then season with salt and pepper.
4. Spoon the mixture into the peppers.
5. Place the steamer insert in the Instant Pot and place the peppers in it.
6. Add the water then close and lock the lid.
7. Press the Manual button and adjust the timer to 15 minutes.
8. When the timer goes off, let the pressure vent naturally.
9. When the pot has depressurized, open the lid and remove the peppers.

Nutrition:

calories 380 fat 24g ,protein 29g ,carbs 10.5g ,fiber 2g ,net carbs 8.5g

Garlic Soy-Glazed Chicken

Prep Time + Cook time:35 minutes , Servings: 6

Ingredients:

- 2 pounds boneless chicken thighs

What you'll need from the store cupboard:

- Salt and pepper
- 1 tablespoon minced garlic
- ¼ cup soy sauce
- ¾ cup apple cider vinegar

Directions:

1. Season the chicken with salt and pepper, then add it to the Instant Pot, skin-side down.
2. Whisk together the apple cider vinegar, soy sauce, and garlic then add to the pot.
3. Close and lock the lid, then press the Manual button and adjust the timer to 15 minutes.
4. When the timer goes off, let the pressure vent naturally.
5. When the pot has depressurized, open the lid.
6. Remove the chicken to a baking sheet and place under the broiler for 3 to 5 minutes until the skin is crisp.
7. Meanwhile, turn the Instant Pot on to Sauté and cook until the sauce thickens, stirring as needed.
8. Serve the chicken with the sauce spooned over it.

Nutrition:

calories 335 fat 23g ,protein 27.5g ,carbs 1.5g ,fiber 0g ,net carbs 1.5g

Italian Turkey Breast with Gravy

Prep Time + Cook time:50 minutes , Servings: 8

Ingredients:

- 1 (4-pound) bone-in turkey breast
- 1 tablespoon coconut flour
- ½ cup chicken broth
- ½ cup whole milk

What you'll need from the store cupboard:

- Salt and pepper
- 1 tablespoon Italian seasoning
- 3 tablespoons butter, divided

Directions:

1. Turn the Instant Pot on to the Sauté setting and let it heat up.
2. Rub 1 tablespoon of the butter into the turkey breast and season with Italian seasoning, salt, and pepper.
3. Add the turkey to the Instant Pot and cook for 2 minutes on each side to brown.
4. Remove the turkey and place the steamer insert in the pot.
5. Add the turkey to the steamer insert, then close and lock the lid.
6. Press the Manual button and adjust the timer to 25 minutes.
7. When the timer goes off, let the pressure vent naturally.
8. When the pot has depressurized, open the lid.
9. Remove the turkey to a cutting board and tent loosely with foil.
10. Add the remaining butter to the pot and whisk in the coconut flour.
11. Press the Sauté button and simmer the sauce for 2 minutes.
12. Whisk in the chicken broth, and milk then cook until thickened, about 3 minutes.
13. Slice the turkey breast and serve with the gravy.

Nutrition:

calories 440 fat 21g ,protein 49g ,carbs 2g ,fiber 1g ,net carbs 1g

Whole Roasted Chicken

Prep Time + Cook time:39 minutes , Servings: 8

Ingredients:

- 1 (4-pound) whole roasting chicken
- 2 teaspoons paprika
- 1 small onion, quartered
- 1 lemon, halved
- 1 cup water

What you'll need from the store cupboard:

- Salt and pepper
- 2 tablespoons butter

Directions:

1. Turn the Instant Pot on to the Sauté setting and let it heat up.
2. Rub the butter into the chicken then season with paprika, salt, and pepper.
3. Place the onion and lemon in the chicken cavity.
4. Add the chicken to the preheated instant pot, skin-side down, and cook for 6 to 7 minutes until browned.
5. Turn the chicken and cook for another 5 minutes, then remove from the pot.
6. Place the trivet inside the Instant Pot and pour it in the water.
7. Place the chicken on the trivet, then close and lock the lid.
8. Press the Manual button and adjust the timer to 24 minutes.
9. When the timer goes off, let the pressure vent for 15 minutes then do a Quick Release by pressing Cancel and switching the steam valve to "venting."
10. When the pot has depressurized, open the lid.
11. Remove the chicken to a cutting board and let rest 10 minutes before carving.

Nutrition:

calories 490 fat 35g ,protein 43g ,carbs 2.5g ,fiber 0.5g ,net carbs 2g

Italian Chicken Stew

Prep Time + Cook time:20 minutes , Servings: 4

Ingredients:

- 1 small yellow onion, chopped
- 1 (14-ounce) can diced tomatoes
- 1 ½ cups chicken broth
- 12 ounces boneless chicken thighs

What you'll need from the store cupboard:

- 1 tablespoon olive oil
- 1 teaspoon dried Italian seasoning
- 1 tablespoon tomato paste

Directions:

1. Turn the Instant Pot on to the Sauté setting and let it heat up.
2. Add the olive oil then sauté the onion for 5 minutes until softened.
3. Add the tomatoes, chicken broth, tomato paste, and seasoning.
4. Stir well then add the chicken and close and lock the lid.
5. Press the Manual button and adjust the timer to 10 minutes on High Pressure.
6. When the timer goes off, let the pressure vent for 10 minutes then do a Quick Release by pressing Cancel and switching the steam valve to "venting."
7. When the pot has depressurized, open the lid.
8. Remove the chicken with a slotted spoon and shred it with two forks.
9. Simmer the cooking liquid on the Sauté setting until it thickens then stir the chicken back in to serve.

Nutrition:

calories 255 fat 17.5g ,protein 18g ,carbs 6.5g ,fiber 1.5g ,net carbs 5g

Chicken Cacciatore

Prep Time + Cook time:20 minutes , Servings: 4

Ingredients:

- 1 ½ pounds boneless chicken thighs, chopped
- 1 (14-ounce) can stewed tomatoes
- 1 small yellow onion, chopped
- ½ cup sliced black olives

What you'll need from the store cupboard:

- 1 tablespoon olive oil
- 2 cloves minced garlic
- 1 teaspoon dried oregano
- Salt and pepper to taste

Directions:

1. Turn the Instant Pot on to the Sauté setting and let it heat up with the oil.
2. Add the chicken and sauté for 3 to 4 minutes until browned.
3. Stir in the tomatoes, onions, garlic, and oregano.
4. Close and lock the lid, then press the Manual button and adjust the timer to 15 minutes.
5. When the timer goes off, let the pressure vent naturally.
6. When the pot has depressurized, open the lid.
7. Stir in the olives and season with salt and pepper. Serve hot.

Nutrition:

calories 440 fat 31g ,protein 31g ,carbs 7g ,fiber 2g ,net carbs 5g

Stewed Chicken and Kale

Prep Time + Cook time:15 minutes , Servings: 4

Ingredients:

- 1 small yellow onion, chopped
- 1 pound boneless chicken thighs, chopped
- 1 (14-ounce) can diced tomatoes
- 1 cup chicken broth
- 3 cups fresh chopped kale

What you'll need from the store cupboard:

- Salt and pepper
- 1 tablespoon butter

Directions:

1. Turn the Instant Pot on to the Sauté setting and let it heat up.
2. Melt the butter in the pot then add the onion.
3. Cook for 3 minutes to soften then stir in the chicken.
4. Add the tomatoes, chicken broth, and kale then season with salt and pepper.
5. Close and lock the lid.
6. Press the Manual button and adjust the timer to 10 minutes.
7. When the timer goes off, let the pressure vent for 10 minutes then do a Quick Release by pressing Cancel and switching the steam valve to "venting."
8. When the pot has depressurized, open the lid.
9. Stir everything together and adjust seasoning to taste.

Nutrition:

calories 325 fat 20.5g ,protein 24g ,carbs 11g ,fiber 2.5g ,net carbs 8.5g

Lemon Garlic Chicken

Prep Time + Cook time:17 minutes , Servings: 8

Ingredients:
- 2 pounds boneless chicken thighs
- 1 small yellow onion, chopped

What you'll need from the store cupboard:
- Salt and pepper
- 2 tablespoons olive oil
- 3 cloves minced garlic
- ¼ cup heavy cream
- ½ cup fresh lemon juice

Directions:
1. Turn the Instant Pot on to the Sauté setting and let it heat up.
2. Heat the oil in the pot then add the chicken – season with salt and pepper.
3. Cook to brown the chicken, about 2 to 3 minutes on each side.
4. Remove the chicken from the pot and add the onion and garlic.
5. Stir in the lemon juice and cook for 1 minute.
6. Add the chicken back to the pot, then close and lock the lid.
7. Press the Manual button and adjust the timer to 7 minutes.
8. When the timer goes off, let the pressure vent for 5 minutes then do a Quick Release by pressing Cancel and switching the steam valve to "venting."
9. When the pot has depressurized, open the lid.
10. Remove the chicken from the pot and stir in the cream.
11. Cook on the Sauté function for 2 to 3 minutes until thickened.
12. Spoon the sauce over the chicken to serve.

Nutrition:
calories 300 fat 22g, protein 20.5g ,carbs 1.5g ,fiber 0.5g ,net carbs 1g

Creamy Salsa Chicken

Prep Time + Cook time:25 minutes , Servings: 6

Ingredients:
- 2 pounds boneless chicken thighs
- 1 tablespoon ground coriander
- 1 cup salsa
- ¼ cup chicken broth

What you'll need from the store cupboard:
- Salt and pepper
- 4 ounces cream cheese, chopped
- 1 tablespoon ground cumin

Directions:
1. Season the chicken with the cumin, coriander, salt, and pepper.
2. Add the chicken to the Instant Pot with the salsa, chicken broth, and cream cheese.
3. Close and lock the lid.
4. Press the Manual button and adjust the timer to 20 minutes on High Pressure.
5. When the timer goes off, let the pressure vent for 15 minutes then do a Quick Release by pressing Cancel and switching the steam valve to "venting."
6. When the pot has depressurized, open the lid.
7. Shred the chicken with two forks and stir everything well. Serve hot.

Nutrition:
calories 400 fat 29.5g ,protein 29g ,carbs 3g ,fiber 0.5g ,net carbs 2.5g

Mustard Chicken with Basil

Prep Time + Cook time: 25 minutes , Servings: 4

5-Ingredients:
- 1 tsp Chicken stock
- 2 Chicken breasts; skinless and boneless chicken breasts: halved
- 1 tbsp Chopped basil

What you'll need from the store cupboard:
- Salt and black pepper
- 1 tbsp Olive oil
- ½ tsp Garlic powder
- ½ tsp Onion powder
- 1 tsp Dijon mustard

Directions:

1. Press 'Sauté' on the instant pot and add the oil. When it is hot, brown the chicken in it for 2-3 minutes.
2. Mix in the remaining ingredients and seal the lid to cook for 12 minutes at high pressure.
3. Natural release the pressure for 10 minutes, share into plates and serve.

Nutrition

Calories 34, fat 3.6, carbs 0.7, protein 0.3, fiber 0.1

Cheesy Chicken And Avocado In Tomato Sauce

Prep Time + Cook time: 27 minutes   , Servings: 8

5-Ingredients:
- 1 cup Shredded cheddar cheese
- 2 Skinless and boneless chicken breast; halved
- 2 Avocados; pitted, peeled and cubed
- 2 cups Tomato passata

What you'll need from the store cupboard:
- A pinch of salt and black pepper
- 1 tbsp Olive oil

Directions:

1. Press 'Sauté' on the instant pot and pour in the oil. When it is hot, brown the chicken for 5 minutes.
2. Mix in the passata, avocados, salt, and pepper.
3. Spread the cheese over the mix and seal the lid to cook for 12minutes at high pressure.
4. Natural release the pressure for 10 minutes, share into plates and serve.

Nutrition

Calories 198, fat 16.4, carbs 6.6, protein 5.4, fiber 4.6

Basil Chili Chicken

Prep Time + Cook time: 25 minutes , Servings: 4

5-Ingredients:
- half cup Chicken stock
- 1 lb. Chicken breast
- 2 tsp Sweet paprika
- 1 cup Coconut cream
- 2 tbsp Basil (sliced)

What you'll need from the store cupboard:
- Salt and Black pepper to taste
- 1 tbsp Chili powder

Directions:

1. In your instant pot, mix the chicken with the other ingredients, then stir them a little, then cover them then heat for 20 minutes on high temperature.

2. Release the pressure gradually for 10 minutes then split them among plates before you eat them.

Nutritional Info per Servings:
Calories: 364, Fat: 23.2, Fiber: 2.3g, Carbs: 5.1g, Protein: 35.4g

Chicken and Oregano Sauce

Prep Time + Cook time: 30 minutes , Servings: 4
5-Ingredients:
- 2 pieces (no skin and bones) Chicken breast
- 1 tbsp Lemon juice
- 1 tsp Ginger
- 2 tbsp Oregano
- 1 cup Tomato passata

What you'll need from the store cupboard:
- 2 tbsp Olive oil

Directions:
1. Put the instant pot on Sauté option, then put the oil and cook it. After that, put the tomato passata and the remaining ingredients except for the chicken then heat it for 5 minutes.
2. Put the other ingredients, then cover it and heat it for 15 minutes on high temperature.
3. Release the pressure gradually for 10 minutes then split them among your containers before eating.

Nutritional Info per Servings:
Calories: 300, Fat: 15.8g, Fiber: 2g, Carbs: 5.2g, Protein: 33.9g

Garlic Chives Chicken

Prep Time + Cook time: 30 minutes , Servings: 4
5-Ingredients:
- 1 lb. (no skin and bones) Chicken breast
- 1 tbsp Chives
- 1 cup Chicken stock
- 1 cup Coconut cream
- 3 tbsp Garlic cloves (sliced)

What you'll need from the store cupboard:
- 1 and a half tbsp Balsamic vinegar
- Salt and Black pepper to taste

Directions:
1. In the instant pot, mix the chicken with all the remaining ingredients, then cover them and cook for 20 minutes on high temperature.
2. Release the pressure gradually for 10 minutes then split them among your plates before eating.

Nutritional Info per Servings:
Calories: 360, Fat: 22.1, Fiber: 1.4g, Carbs: 4.1g, Protein: 34.5g

Oregano Flavored Chicken Olives

Prep Time + Cook time: 30 minutes , Servings: 4
5-Ingredients:
- 2 pieces (without skin and bones) Chicken breasts
- 2 pieces Eggplants
- 1 tbsp Oregano
- 1 cup Tomato passata

What you'll need from the store cupboard:
- Salt and Black pepper to taste
- 2 tbsp Olive oil

Directions:
1. In the instant pot mix all the ingredients, then cover them and cook for 20 minutes on high temperature.

2. Release the pressure gradually for 10 minutes then split them among your plates before eating.

Nutritional Info per Servings:
Calories: 362, Fat: 16.1, Fiber: 4.4g, Carbs: 5.4g, Protein: 36.4g

Turkey and Spring Onions Mix

Prep Time + Cook time: 25 minutes , Servings: 4
5-Ingredients:
- Cilantro
- 4 pieces Spring onions (sliced)
- 1 piece (no skin and bones) Turkey breast
- 1 cup Tomato passata

What you'll need from the store cupboard:
- 2 tbsp Avocado oil
- Salt and Black pepper to taste

Directions:

1. Put the instant pot on Sauté option, then put the oil and cook it. After that, put the meat then heat it for 5 minutes.
2. Put the other ingredients, then cover it and heat it for 20 minutes on high temperature.
3. Release the pressure gradually for 10 minutes then split them among your plates before eating.

Nutritional Info per Servings:
Calories: 222, Fat: 6.7g, Fiber: 1.6g, Carbs: 4.8g, Protein: 34.4g

Sweet and Chili Turkey Breast

Prep Time + Cook time: 35 minutes , Servings: 4
5-Ingredients:
- 2 tbsp Cilantro
- 1 lb. Brussels sprouts
- 1 piece (large, no skin and bones) Turkey breast
- 1 and a half cup Tomato passata

What you'll need from the store cupboard:
- 1 tbsp Avocado oil
- Salt and Black pepper to taste
- 1 tsp Chili powder

Directions:

1. Put the instant pot on Sauté option, then put the oil and cook it. After that, put the meat then heat it for 5 minutes.
2. Put the other ingredients, then cover it and heat it for 20 minutes on high temperature.
3. Release the pressure gradually for 10 minutes then split them among your plates before eating.

Nutritional Info per Servings:
Calories: 249, Fat: 6.6g, Fiber: 2.5g, Carbs: 4.5g, Protein: 37.3g

Peppered Broccoli Chicken

Prep Time + Cook time: 30 minutes , Servings: 4
5-Ingredients:
- 1 tbsp Sage (sliced)
- 1 cup Broccoli florets
- 1 lb. (no bones and skin) Chicken breast
- 3 pieces Garlic cloves
- 1 cup Tomato passata

What you'll need from the store cupboard:
- Salt and Black pepper to taste
- 2 tbsp. Olive oil

Directions:

1. Put the instant pot on Sauté option, then put the oil and cook it. After that, put the chicken and garlic then heats it for 5 minutes.
2. Put the other ingredients, then cover it and heat it for 25 minutes on high temperature.
3. Release the pressure gradually for 10 minutes then split them among your plates before eating.

Nutritional Info per Servings:
Calories: 217, Fat: 10.1g, Fiber: 1.8g, Carbs: 5.9g, Protein: 25.4g

Turkey in Tomato Puree

Prep Time + Cook time: 40 minutes , Servings: 4
5-Ingredients:
- 2 tbsp Tomato puree
- 1 cup Chicken stock
- 1 cup Shredded red cabbage
- 2 pieces (no skin and bones) Turkey breasts
- 1 Chopped spring onion

What you'll need from the store cupboard:
- 1 tbsp olive oil
- Salt and Black pepper to taste
- half tsp. Chili powder
- 2 cloves Minced garlic

Directions:
1. Press 'Sauté' on the instant pot with olive oil, add onion and cabbage. When it is hot, mix in the turkey breast and garlic to brown for 5 minutes.
2. Add the tomato puree, seasoning, chicken stock and chili powder to the pot and seal the lid to cook for 20 minutes at high pressure.
3. Natural release the pressure for 10 minutes, share into bowls and serve.

Nutritional Info per Servings:
Calories: 392, Fat: 11.6g, Fiber: 0.3g, Carbs: 1.1g, Protein: 24.2g

Spinach and Garlic Flavored Chicken

Prep Time + Cook time: 35 minutes , Servings: 4
5-Ingredients:
- 2 tbsp Cilantro
- 1 cup Chicken stock
- 1 lb. (no bones and skin) Chicken breasts
- 1 lb. Baby spinach
- 3 pieces Garlic cloves

What you'll need from the store cupboard:
- Salt and Black pepper to taste
- 2 tbsp Melted ghee

Directions:
1. Put the instant pot on Sauté option, then put the ghee and cook it. After that, put the meat and garlic then heat it for 5 minutes.
2. Put the other ingredients except for the spinach, then cover it and heat it for 15 minutes on high temperature.
3. Release the pressure gradually for 10 minutes. After that, put the instant pot on Sauté option once more, then put the spinach, heat for an additional 5 minutes, then split them among your plates before eating.

Nutritional Info per Servings:
Calories: 304, Fat: 15.4g, Fiber: 2.6g, Carbs: 5.1g, Protein: 36.4g

Turkey Coriander Dish

Prep Time + Cook time: 40 minutes , Servings: 4

5-Ingredients:

- half bunch Coriander (sliced)
- 1 cup Chard (sliced)
- 1 piece (no bones and skin) Turkey breast
- 1 and a half cup Coconut cream
- 2 pieces Garlic cloves

What you'll need from the store cupboard:

- 1 tbsp Melted ghee

Directions:

1. Put the instant pot on Sauté option, then put the ghee and cook it. After that, put the garlic and meat then heat it for 5 minutes.
2. Put the other ingredients, then cover it and heat it for 25 minutes on high temperature.
3. Release the pressure gradually for 10 minutes then split them among your plates before eating.

Nutritional Info per Servings:

Calories: 225, Fat: 8.9g, Fiber: 0.2g, Carbs: 0.8g, Protein: 33.5g

Duck with Garlic and Onion Sauce

Prep Time + Cook time: 40 minutes , Servings: 4

5-Ingredients:

- 2 tbsp Coriander
- 2 pieces Spring onions
- 1 lb. (no skin and bones) Duck legs
- 2 pieces Garlic cloves
- 2 tbsp Tomato passata

What you'll need from the store cupboard:

- 2 tbsp Melted ghee

Directions:

1. Put the instant pot on Sauté option, then put the ghee and cook it. After that, put the spring onions and the other ingredients excluding the tomato passata and the meat then heat it for 5 minutes.
2. Put the meat and cook for 5 minutes.
3. Put the sauce then cover it and heat it for 25 minutes on high temperature.
4. Release the pressure gradually for 10 minutes then split them among your plates before eating.

Nutritional Info per Servings:

Calories: 263, Fat: 13.2g, Fiber: 0.2g, Carbs: 1.1g, Protein: 33.5g

Salty Turkey Chives

Prep Time + Cook time: 40 minutes , Servings: 4

5-Ingredients:

- 1 tbsp Chives (sliced)
- 1 cup Chicken stock
- 1 cup Salsa verde
- 1 piece (no skin and bones) Large turkey breast

What you'll need from the store cupboard:

- Salt and Black pepper to taste

Directions:

1. In the instant pot, combine all the ingredients then cover them, then stir and cook for 30 minutes on high temperature.
2. Release the pressure gradually for 10 minutes then split them among your plates before eating.

Nutritional Info per Servings:

Calories: 211, Fat: 9.2g, Fiber: 6g, Carbs: 0.3g, Protein: 34.5g

Cilantro Duck Dish with Turmeric Flavor

Prep Time + Cook time: 35 minutes , Servings: 4

5-Ingredients:

- 1 tbsp Cilantro (sliced)
- 1 cup Chicken stock
- 1 lb. (no bones and skin) Duck legs
- 1 piece Shallot (sliced)
- 2 pieces Garlic cloves

What you'll need from the store cupboard:

- Salt and Black pepper to taste
- 1 tbsp Olive oil
- 1 tsp Turmeric powder

Directions:

1. Set your instant pot on Sauté mode, add the oil, heat it and add the shallot, garlic and the meat and brown for 5 minutes.
2. Add the rest of the ingredients except the cilantro, put the lid on and cook on High for 25 minutes.
3. Release the pressure fast for 5 minutes, divide the mix between plates and serve with the cilantro sprinkled on top.

Nutritional Info per Servings:

Calories: 239, Fat: 10.5g, Fiber: 0.2g, Carbs: 1.1g, Protein: 33.3g

Peppered Chicken Breast with Basil

Prep Time + Cook time: 30 minutes , Servings: 4

5-Ingredients:

- ¼ cup Red bell peppers
- 1 cup Chicken stock
- 2 pieces (no skin and bones) Chicken breasts
- 4 pieces Garlic cloves (crushed)
- 1 and a half tbsp Basil (crushed)

What you'll need from the store cupboard:

- 1 tbsp Chili powder

Directions:

1. In the instant pot, combine the ingredients then cover them and cook for 25 minutes on high temperature.
2. Release the pressure quickly for 5 minutes then split them among your plates before eating.

Nutritional Info per Servings:

Calories: 230, Fat: 12.4g, Fiber: 0.8g, Carbs: 2.7g, Protein: 33.2g

Chicken in Coconut Cream

Prep Time + Cook time: 40 minutes , Servings: 4

5-Ingredients:

- ¼ cup Cilantro
- 1 cup Chicken stock
- 2 tsp Garam masala
- 2 pieces (no skin and bones) Chicken breasts
- 1 cup Coconut cream

What you'll need from the store cupboard:

- Salt and Black pepper to taste

Directions:

1. In the instant pot, combine the ingredients with the chicken, then cover them and cook for 30 minutes on high temperature.
2. Release the pressure rapidly for 10 minutes then split them among your plates before eating.

Nutritional Info per Servings:

Calories: 356, Fat: 22.9g, Fiber: 1.4g, Carbs: 3.6g, Protein: 34.4g

Coco Turkey in Tomato Passata

Prep Time + Cook time: 35 minutes , Servings: 4

5-Ingredients:
- 1 piece (no bones and skin) Large turkey
- 1 and a half cups Coconut cream
- 2 tbsp Garlic
- 1 tsp Basil
- 2 tbsp Tomato passata

What you'll need from the store cupboard:
- Salt and Black pepper to taste
- 1 tbsp Melted ghee

Directions:
1. Put the instant pot on Sauté option, then put the ghee and cook it. After that, put the garlic and meat then heat it for 5 minutes.
2. Put the other ingredients then cover it and heat it for 20 minutes on high temperature.
3. Release the pressure gradually for 10 minutes, then after that split them among your plates before eating.

Nutritional Info per Servings:
Calories: 229, Fat: 8.9g, Fiber: 0.2g, Carbs: 1.8g, Protein: 33.6g

Mozzarella Flavored Turkey

Prep Time + Cook time: 35 minutes , Servings: 4

5-Ingredients:
- 1 tbsp Cilantro (sliced)
- 1 cup Chicken stock
- 1 cup Mozzarella (grated)
- 1 piece (no bones and skin) Turkey breast

What you'll need from the store cupboard:
- 1 tbsp Avocado oil
- 1 tsp Chili powder
- 2 cups Bell peppers

Directions:
1. Put the instant pot on Sauté option, then put the oil and cook it. Afterward, place the chili powder and meat and cook them for about 5 minutes.
2. Put the other ingredients excluding the mozzarella and cilantro, then stir slowly.
3. Put the mozzarella on its surface, then cover it and heat it for 20 minutes on high heat.
4. Release the pressure slowly for 10 minutes, then split them among plates and consume with cilantro as a topping.

Nutritional Info per Servings:
Calories: 222, Fat: 7.6g, Fiber: 0.4g, Carbs: 1g, Protein: 35.5g

Coco Flavored Duck Legs

Prep Time + Cook time: 40 minutes , Servings: 6

5-Ingredients:
- 1 cup Chicken stock
- half cup Unsweetened coconut
- 2 pieces Large duck legs
- 1 cup Coconut cream

What you'll need from the store cupboard:
- Salt and Black pepper to taste
- 1 tbsp Olive oil
- 1 tbsp Thyme

Directions:
1. Put the instant pot on Sauté option, then put the oil and cook it. After that, put the meat then heat it for 5 minutes.
2. Put the other ingredients, then cover it and heat it for 25 minutes on high temperature.

3. Release the pressure gradually for 10 minutes, then after that split them among your plates and serve.

Chick n' Kale in Basil

Prep Time + Cook time: 60 minutes , Servings: 4
5-Ingredients:
- 1 cup Chicken stock
- 2 cups Kale (crushed)
- 2 pieces (no bones and skin) Chicken breasts

What you'll need from the store cupboard:
- Salt and Black pepper to taste
- 2 tbsp Melted ghee
- 1 tbsp Tabasco sauce
- 1 tbsp Basil

Directions:
1. In the instant pot, combine seasoning with the chicken, then cover them and cook for 25 minutes on high temperature.
2. Release the pressure rapidly for 10 minutes then split them among your plates before eating.
3. Put the instant pot on Sauté option, then put the oil and cook it. After that, put the meat then heat it for 5 minutes.
4. Put the other ingredients and heat it for 20 minutes at high temperature.
5. Release the pressure gradually for 10 minutes, then after that split them among your plates before eating.

Cheesy Turkey

Prep Time + Cook time: 40 minutes , Servings: 6
5-Ingredients:
- 1 cup Cheddar cheese (shredded)
- 1 piece (no bones and skin) Large turkey
- 1 cup Coconut milk
- 4 pieces Garlic cloves (sliced)

What you'll need from the store cupboard:
- Salt and Black pepper to taste
- 1 tbsp Olive oil
- 1 tbsp Ginger (shredded)

Directions:
1. Put the instant pot on Sauté option, then put the oil and cook it. After that, put the ginger, turkey, and the garlic then heat it for 5 minutes.
2. Put the other ingredients excluding the cheese and stir.
3. Put the cheese at the uppermost surface, then cover it and heat it for 25 minutes on high temperature.
4. Release the pressure gradually for 10 minutes, then after that split them among your plates before eating.

Nutty Chicken Dish

Prep Time + Cook time: 30 minutes , Servings: 4

5-Ingredients:
- 1 tbsp Chives
- 2 tbsp Almonds (crushed)
- 2 pieces (no bones and skin) Chicken breasts
- 1 cup Chicken stock

What you'll need from the store cupboard:
- 2 tbsp Avocado oil
- Salt and Black pepper to taste
- 1 tbsp Balsamic vinegar

Directions:

1. Put the instant pot on Sauté option, then put the oil and cook it. After that, put the chicken then heat it for 5 minutes.
2. Put the other ingredients, then cover it and heat it for 20 minutes on high temperature.
3. Release the pressure quickly for 5 minutes, then after that split them among your plates before eating.

Nutritional Info per Servings:
Calories: 254, Fat: 11.7g, Fiber: 0.9g, Carbs: 1.6g, Protein: 3.4g

Turkey, Brussels Sprouts and Walnuts

Prep Time + Cook time: 30 minutes , Servings: 4

5-Ingredients:
- 1 tbsp Walnuts
- 1 lb. Brussels sprouts (grated)
- 1 piece Turkey breast (large)

What you'll need from the store cupboard:
- Salt and Black pepper to taste
- 2 tbsp Olive oil
- 1 tbsp Chili powder
- 1 tbsp Garlic (sliced)

Directions:

1. Put the instant pot on Sauté option, then put the oil and cook it. After that, put the turkey then heat it for 5 minutes.
2. Put the other ingredients then cover it and heat it for 20 minutes on high temperature.
3. Release the pressure quickly for 5 minutes, then after that split them among your plates before eating.

Nutritional Info per Servings:
Calories: 323, Fat: 14.5g, Fiber: 5.4g, Carbs: 6.3g, Protein: 34.9g

Chapter 6 Beef, Lamb Pork Recipes

Easy Beef Bourguignon

Prep Time + Cook time:40 minutes , Servings: 6

Ingredients:

- 1 pound beef stew meat, chopped
- 8 slices bacon, chopped
- 1 small yellow onion, chopped
- 1 ½ cups beef broth

What you'll need from the store cupboard:

- Salt and pepper
- 1 ½ tablespoons olive oil
- 3 cloves minced garlic

Directions:

1. Turn the Instant Pot on to the Sauté setting and let it heat up.
2. Add the oil then season the beef with salt and pepper and add it to the pot.
3. Cook for 4 to 5 minutes until browned, stirring often.
4. Add the bacon, onions, and garlic and cook for 4 minutes, stirring.
5. Stir in the beef broth then season with salt and pepper.
6. Close and lock the lid on the Instant Pot.
7. Press the Manual button and adjust the timer to 30 minutes.
8. When the timer goes off, let the pressure vent naturally.
9. When the pot has depressurized, open the lid.
10. Stir well and adjust seasoning to taste. Serve hot.

Nutrition:

calories 255 fat 14g ,protein 29g ,carbs 2g ,fiber 0.5g ,net carbs 1.5g

Shredded Beef

Prep Time + Cook time:1 hour 30 minutes , Servings: 6

Ingredients:

- 3 pounds boneless beef rump roast
- 1 ¼ cups beef broth

What you'll need from the store cupboard:

- Salt and pepper
- 2 tablespoons olive oil
- 1 teaspoon dried oregano
- 1 teaspoon dried basil
- 1 teaspoon dried thyme

Directions:

1. Turn the Instant Pot on to the Sauté setting and let it heat up.
2. Add the oil to the pot and season the beef with salt and pepper.
3. Add the beef and cook for 2 minutes on each side until browned.
4. Whisk together the remaining ingredients and pour into the pot with the beef.
5. Close and lock the lid.
6. Press the Manual button and adjust the timer to 75 minutes.
7. When the timer goes off, let the pressure vent naturally. When the pot has depressurized, open the lid.
8. Shred the beef with two forks and stir into the cooking liquid.

Nutrition:

calories 455 fat 18.5g ,protein 71.5g ,carbs 0.5g ,fiber 0g ,net carbs 0.5g

Braised Beef Short Ribs

Prep Time + Cook time:50 minutes , Servings: 8

Ingredients:

- 2 pounds boneless beef short ribs
- 1 small yellow onion, chopped
- 1 tablespoon Worcestershire sauce

What you'll need from the store cupboard:

- Salt and pepper
- 1 tablespoon olive oil
- ¼ cup tomato paste
- ½ cup red wine

Directions:

1. Turn the Instant Pot on to the Sauté setting and let it heat up.
2. Add the oil to the pot and season the short ribs with salt and pepper.
3. Place the ribs in the pot and cook for 2 minutes on each side to brown.
4. Remove the ribs then add the onions to the pot and cook for 5 minutes.
5. Stir in the garlic then add the rest of the ingredients, including the ribs.
6. Close and lock the lid, then press the Manual button and adjust the timer to 35 minutes.
7. When the timer goes off, let the pressure vent for 5 minutes then do a Quick Release by pressing Cancel and switching the steam valve to "venting."
8. When the pot has depressurized, open the lid. Remove the ribs to serve.

Nutrition:

calories 480 fat 43g ,protein 16.5g ,carbs 3g ,fiber 0.5g ,net carbs 2.5g

Classic Meatloaf

Prep Time + Cook time:45 minutes , Servings: 8

Ingredients:

- 2 pounds ground beef (80% lean)
- 1 cup grated parmesan cheese
- 3 large eggs

What you'll need from the store cupboard:

- Salt and pepper
- 1 tablespoon minced garlic
- 1 teaspoon dried oregano
- 1 cup almond flour

Directions:

1. Combine the ground beef, almond flour, parmesan cheese, eggs, garlic, and oregano in a bowl.
2. Mix well by hand then season with salt and pepper.
3. Place the steamer rack in your Instant Pot and line with foil.
4. Shape the meat mixture into a loaf and place it on the foil, close and lock the lid.
5. Press the Manual button and adjust the timer to 35 minutes.
6. When the timer goes off, do a Quick Release by pressing Cancel and switching the steam valve to "venting."
7. When the pot has depressurized, open the lid.
8. Remove the meatloaf to a roasting pan and broil for 5 minutes to brown before slicing to serve.

Nutrition:

calories 460 fat 31g ,protein 39.5g ,carbs 3g ,fiber 1.5g

Korean BBQ Beef

Prep Time + Cook time:25 minutes , Servings: 6

Ingredients:

- 3 pounds boneless beef chuck roast, cut into chunks

What you'll need from the store cupboard:

- Salt and pepper
- 3 cloves minced garlic
- 1 tablespoon fresh grated ginger
- 1/3 cup soy sauce
- 2 tablespoons rice wine vinegar
- 6 tablespoons powdered erythritol

Directions:

1. Whisk together the soy sauce, powdered erythritol, ginger, garlic, and rice wine vinegar in a bowl.
2. Season the beef with salt and pepper then place it in the Instant Pot.
3. Pour the sauce over it then close and lock the lid.
4. Press the Manual button and adjust the timer to 15 minutes.
5. When the timer goes off, do a Quick Release by pressing Cancel and switching the steam valve to "venting."
6. When the pot has depressurized, open the lid. Serve the beef hot.

Nutrition:

calories 440 fat 14g ,protein 70g ,carbs 2.5g ,fiber 0.5g ,net carbs 2g

Bolognese Sauce

Prep Time + Cook time:40 minutes , Servings: 8

Ingredients:

- 1 small yellow onion, chopped
- 1 pound ground beef (80% lean)
- ¼ pound chopped bacon
- 2 (14-ounce) cans crushed tomatoes
- ½ cup water

What you'll need from the store cupboard:

- 1 tablespoon olive oil
- ¼ cup heavy cream
- 2 tablespoons tomato paste
- Salt and pepper to taste

Directions:

1. Turn the Instant Pot on to the Sauté setting and let it heat up.
2. Add the oil to the pot and add the onions – sauté for 4 to 5 minutes.
3. Stir in the beef and bacon then cook until browned, about 10 minutes.
4. Stir in the tomato paste and cook 1 minute more than pour in the wine.
5. Add tomatoes and ½ cup water, bring to a simmer, then close and lock the lid.
6. Press the Manual button and adjust the timer to 20 minutes.
7. When the timer goes off, do a Quick Release by pressing Cancel and switching the steam valve to "venting."
8. When the pot has depressurized, open the lid.
9. Stir in the heavy cream and adjust the seasoning to taste.
10. Press the Sauté button and simmer until the sauce has thickened and serve over zucchini noodles.

Nutrition:

calories 305 fat 19g ,protein 23g ,carbs 10g ,fiber 3.5g ,net carbs 6.5g

Stewed Beef with Mushrooms

Prep Time + Cook time:32 minutes , Servings: 6

Ingredients:

- 2 pounds beef stew meat, chopped
- 10 ounces sliced mushrooms
- 3 cups beef broth
- ¼ cup water

What you'll need from the store cupboard:

- Salt and pepper
- 1 ½ tablespoons olive oil
- 2 cloves minced garlic
- 2 tablespoons almond flour

Directions:

1. Turn the Instant Pot on to the Sauté setting and let it heat up.
2. Add the oil to the pot and season the beef with salt and pepper.
3. Add the beef to the pot and cook for 4 to 5 minutes until browned.
4. Stir in the mushrooms and garlic and cook for 3 to 4 minutes.
5. Stir in the almond flour and ¼ cup water, scraping up the browned bits.
6. Add the beef broth then close and lock the lid.
7. Press the Manual button and adjust the timer to 5 minutes.
8. When the timer goes off, let the pressure vent for 10 minutes then do a Quick Release by pressing Cancel and switching the steam valve to "venting."
9. When the pot has depressurized, open the lid.
10. Stir everything together well then serve hot.

Nutrition:

calories 355 fat 15g ,protein 50g ,carbs 3g ,fiber 1g ,net carbs 2g

Beef and Chorizo Chili

Prep Time + Cook time:25 minutes , Servings: 6

Ingredients:

- ½ pound diced chorizo sausage
- 1 small yellow onion, chopped
- 1 pound ground beef (80% lean)
- 2 cups diced tomatoes

What you'll need from the store cupboard:

- Salt and pepper
- 1 tablespoon olive oil
- 3 cloves minced garlic

Directions:

1. Turn the Instant Pot on to the Sauté setting and let it heat up.
2. Add the oil to the pot and season the beef with salt and pepper.
3. Stir in the chorizo and onion and cook for 4 to 5 minutes until the chorizo is browned.
4. Add the beef and garlic then season with salt and pepper – cook for 3 minutes.
5. Stir in the tomatoes then close and lock the lid.
6. Press the Manual button and adjust the timer to 15 minutes.
7. When the timer goes off, let the pressure vent for 5 minutes then do a Quick Release by pressing Cancel and switching the steam valve to "venting."
8. When the pot has depressurized, open the lid. Stir well and serve hot.

Nutrition:

calories 370 fat 26g ,protein 28.5g ,carbs 4g ,fiber 1g ,net carbs 3g

Quick and Easy Taco Meat

Prep Time + Cook time:28 minutes , Servings: 8

Ingredients:

- 1 small yellow onion, diced
- 2 pounds ground beef (80% lean)

What you'll need from the store cupboard:

- 2 tablespoons olive oil
- 1 teaspoon garlic powder
- 2 teaspoons dried oregano
- ½ tablespoon chili powder
- Salt amd pepper

Directions:

1. Turn the Instant Pot on to the Sauté setting and let it heat up.
2. Add the oil to the pot along with the seasonings.
3. Cook for 5 minutes, stirring often, then stir in the onion and ground beef.
4. Sauté for 3 to 4 minutes then close and lock the lid.
5. Press the Manual button and adjust the timer to 10 minutes.
6. When the timer goes off, let the pressure vent for 10 minutes then do a Quick Release by pressing Cancel and switching the steam valve to "venting."
7. When the pot has depressurized, open the lid.
8. Stir everything together and serve hot.

Nutrition:

calories 345 fat 23g ,protein 31g ,carbs 1.5g ,fiber 0.5g ,net carbs 1g

Balsamic Beef Pot Roast

Prep Time + Cook time:45 minutes , Servings: 8

Ingredients:

- 3 pounds boneless beef chuck roast
- 1 small yellow onion
- 2 cups water

What you'll need from the store cupboard:

- Salt and pepper
- 1 tablespoon olive oil
- ¼ cup balsamic vinegar
- ¼ teaspoon xanthan gum

Directions:

1. Turn the Instant Pot on to the Sauté setting and let it heat up.
2. Add the oil to the pot and season the beef with salt and pepper.
3. Place the beef in the pot (you may need to cut it into two pieces) and cook for 2 to 3 minutes on each side to brown.
4. Sprinkle in the onions then pour in the water and balsamic vinegar.
5. Close and lock the lid, then press the Manual button and adjust the timer to 40 minutes.
6. When the timer goes off, do a Quick Release by pressing Cancel and switching the steam valve to "venting."
7. When the pot has depressurized, open the lid.
8. Remove the beef to a bowl and break it up into pieces while you simmer the cooking liquid on the Sauté setting.
9. Whisk in the xanthan gum and simmer until thickened.
10. Stir the beef back into the sauce and serve hot.

Nutrition:

calories 335 fat 12.5g ,protein 52g ,carbs 1g ,fiber 0.5g ,net carbs 0.5g

60

Zesty Beef Bites

Prep time + Cook time: 25 minutes , Servings: 4

5-Ingredients:

- 1 pound (cubed) Beef stew meat
- 1 tbsp (grated) Lime zest
- 1 cup Beef stock
- 2 (minced) Garlic cloves
- 1 tbsp (chopped) Oregano

What you'll need from the store cupboard:

- 2 tbsp Avocado oil
- 1 tbsp Lime juice
- 1 tbsp Smoked paprika

Directions:

1. Let your Instant Pot preheat on Sauté mode.
2. Add oil, and meat, then sauté for 5 minutes.
3. Stir in remaining ingredients and mix well
4. Seal the pot's lid and cook for 10 minutes on manual mode at High.
5. Allow the pressure to release in 10 minutes naturally then remove the lid.
6. Serve fresh and enjoy.

Nutrition:
Calories 236, Total Fat: 8.4g, Carbs: 2.8g, Protein: 34.5g, Fiber: 1.6g.

Cheesy Beef with Tomato Sauce

Prep Time + Cook time: 40 minutes , Servings: 6

5-Ingredients:

- 2 lb. Cubed beef
- 2 cups Shredded cheddar cheese
- 1 cup Chicken stock
- ½ cup Okra
- 3 Chopped spring onions

What you'll need from the store cupboard:

- A pinch of salt and black pepper
- 1 tbsp Olive oil
- 2 tbsp Mustard
- 1 cup Tomato passata

Directions:

1. Press 'Sauté' on the instant pot and add the oil. When hot, add brown the meat in the oil for 5 minutes.
2. Mix in the mustard, passata, chicken stock, okra, spring onions, salt, and pepper and seal the lid to cook for 15 minutes at high pressure.
3. Natural release the pressure for 10 minutes and spread the cheese over the beef mix and set aside for 10 minutes, then share into bowls and serve.

Nutrition
Calories 411, fat 19.3, carbs 5, protein 52.4, fiber 1.6

Cheesy Garlic Beef Bowls

Prep Time + Cook time: 30 minutes , Servings: 6

5-Ingredients:

- 2 lb Thinly sliced beef roast
- 1 cup Crumbled feta cheese
- 1 tbsp Chopped parsley
- ½ cup Veggie stock
- 3 cloves Minced garlic

What you'll need from the store cupboard:

- A pinch of salt and black pepper
- 1 tsp Balsamic vinegar
- 2 tbsp Olive oil

Directions:

1. Press 'Sauté' on the instant pot and pour in the oil. When hot, brown the garlic and the meat for 5 minutes.
2. Mix in the vinegar, garlic, stock, salt, and pepper, seal the lid and cook for 15 minutes at high pressure.
3. Natural release the pressure for 10 minutes, then spread the cheese over it and share into plates and serve.

Nutrition

Calories 390, fat 19.4, carbs 1.6, protein 9.5, fiber 0.1

Creamy Lime Turkey with Tomato Sauce

Prep Time + Cook time: 35 minutes, Servings: 4

5-Ingredients:
- 1 Skinless and boneless turkey breasts; cubed
- 1 tbsp Garam masala
- 1 cup Greek yogurt
- 1 tbsp Lime juice
- ¼ tsp Grated ginger

What you'll need from the store cupboard:
- A pinch of salt and black pepper
- 1 tbsp Avocado oil
- 1 cup Tomato passata

Directions:

1. Press 'Sauté' on the instant pot and add the oil. When hot, mix in the garam masala, turkey, and ginger to brown for 5 minutes.
2. Mix in the remaining ingredients and seal the lid to cook for 20 minutes at high pressure.
3. Natural release the pressure for 10 minutes, share the mix and serve.

Nutrition

Calories 20, fat 4.6, carbs 3.6, protein 0.9, fiber 1.1

Balsamic Pork Tenderloin

Prep Time + Cook time:45 minutes , Servings: 6

Ingredients:
- ¼ cup water
- 1 (2-pound) boneless pork tenderloin

What you'll need from the store cupboard:
- Salt and pepper
- 1 tablespoon olive oil
- 3 tablespoons powdered erythritol
- ¼ cup balsamic vinegar

Directions:
1. Turn the Instant Pot on to the Sauté setting and let it heat up.
2. Meanwhile, whisk together the water, balsamic vinegar, and powdered erythritol.
3. Add the oil to the pot and the pork tenderloin. Season with salt and pepper.
4. Cook the pork until it is browned on all sides, rotating as needed, about 8 minutes total.
5. Pour in the sauce then close and lock the lid.
6. Press the Meat/Stew button and adjust the timer for 35 minutes.
7. When the timer goes off, let the pressure vent naturally.
8. When the pot has depressurized, open the lid. Slice the pork to serve.

Nutrition:

calories 160 fat 4g ,protein 28g ,carbs 1.5g ,fiber 0g ,net carbs 1.5g

Spicy Garlic Pork and Okra Jumble

Prep Time + Cook time: 40 minutes , Servings: 4

5-Ingredients:

- 2 lbs. Cubed pork sirloin
- 1 ½ cups Okra
- 2 cloves Minced garlic

What you'll need from the store cupboard:

- A pinch of salt and black pepper
- 1 tbsp Olive oil
- 1 tbsp Smoked paprika
- 1 cup Tomato passata

Directions:

1. Press 'Sauté' on the instant pot and add the oil. When hot, brown the garlic, salt, pepper, and the meat for 5 minutes.
2. Mix in the rest of the ingredients and seal the lid to cook for 25 minutes at high pressure.
3. Natural release the pressure for 10 minutes, share into bowls and serve.

Nutrition

Calories 66, fat 3.9, carbs 2.7, protein 1.6, fiber 2

Braised Lamb Chops

Prep Time + Cook time:12 minutes , Servings: 4

Ingredients:

- 8 bone-in lamb chops (about 2 pounds)
- 1 small yellow onion, diced
- 1 cup beef broth

What you'll need from the store cupboard:

- Salt and pepper
- 1 tablespoon olive oil
- ¼ cup low-carb tomato sauce

Directions:

1. Turn the Instant Pot on to the Sauté setting and let it heat up.
2. Add the oil to the pot and season the lamb with salt and pepper.
3. Add the lamb to the pot and cook for 1 to 2 minutes on each side to brown.
4. Remove the lamb chops and add the onion and tomato sauce to the pot.
5. Cook for 2 minutes then stir in the beef broth.
6. Add the lamb then close and lock the lid.
7. Press the Manual button and adjust the timer for 2 minutes.
8. When the timer goes off, do a Quick Release by pressing Cancel and switching the steam valve to "venting."
9. When the pot has depressurized, open the lid.
10. Spoon the lamb and sauce into a serving bowl and serve hot.

Nutrition:

calories 350 fat 16g ,protein 47.5g ,carbs 2.5g ,fiber 0.5g ,net carbs 2g

Lamb in Tomato Sauce with Olives

Prep Time + Cook time: 40 minutes , Servings: 4

5-Ingredients:

- 1 ½ lbs. Lamb shoulder; cubed
- 1 cup Beef stock
- 1 cup Black olives; pitted and sliced
- 2 Cubed tomatoes

What you'll need from the store cupboard:

- A pinch of salt and black pepper
- 1 tbsp Avocado oil
- 2 tbsp Chopped basil
- 1 cup Tomato passata

Directions:

1. Press 'Sauté' on the instant pot and add the oil. When hot, brown the lamb meat for 5 minutes.
2. Mix in the passata, beef stock, olives, tomatoes, salt and pepper, then seal the lid to cook for 25 minutes at high pressure.
3. Natural release the pressure for 10 minutes, dish into bowls and serve topped with basil.

Nutrition

Calories 251, fat 5.6, carbs 4.7, protein 8.3, fiber 2.7

Chili Lamb And Zucchini In Tomato Sauce

Prep Time + Cook time: 40 minutes , Servings: 4

5-Ingredients:

- 1 tbsp Chopped dill
- ¼ cup Veggie stock
- 2 Slice zucchini
- 1 lb. Lamb shoulder; cubed

What you'll need from the store cupboard:

- A pinch of salt and black pepper
- 2 tbsp Olive oil
- 1 tsp Sweet paprika
- 2 tbsp Tomato passata

Directions:

1. Press 'Sauté' on the instant pot and add the oil. When hot, brown the lamb for 5 minutes.
2. Mix in the remaining ingredients and seal the lid to cook for 25 minutes at high pressure.
3. Natural release the pressure for 10 minutes, share into bowls and serve.

Nutrition

Calories 292, fat 15.6, carbs 4.5, protein 33.4, fiber 1.5

Easy Lamb with Gravy

Prep Time + Cook time:1hour 40 minutes , Servings: 5

Ingredients:

- 2 pounds boneless leg of lamb
- 1 ½ cups water
- 2 tablespoons coconut flour

What you'll need from the store cupboard:

- Salt and pepper
- 1 tablespoon olive oil
- 1 teaspoon dried oregano
- ½ cup white wine

Directions:

1. Turn the Instant Pot on to the Sauté setting and let it heat up.
2. Add the oil to the pot and season the lamb with oregano, salt, and pepper.
3. Place the lamb in the pot and cook for 2 to 3 minutes on each side to brown.
4. Pour in the wine and let it simmer for a few minutes then pour in the water.
5. Add the lamb then close and lock the lid.
6. Press the Manual button and cook on High Pressure for 90 minutes.
7. When the timer goes off, let the pressure vent for 20 minutes then do a Quick Release by pressing Cancel and switching the steam valve to "venting."
8. When the pot has depressurized, open the lid.
9. Remove the lamb to a cutting board and keep warm.
10. Press the Sauté button and whisk the coconut flour into the cooking liquid.
11. Cook for 5 minutes or until thickened the season with salt and pepper.
12. Serve the gravy with the lamb.

Nutrition:

calories 405 fat 17g ,protein 52g ,carbs 4g ,fiber 2g ,net carbs 2g

Spicy Pork Carnitas

Prep Time + Cook time: 55 minutes , Servings: 10

Ingredients:

- ¼ teaspoon cayenne
- 5 pounds boneless pork shoulder, cut into large pieces
- 1 cup water

What you'll need from the store cupboard:

- Salt and pepper
- 2 teaspoons ground cumin
- 1 tablespoon chili powder

Directions:

1. Combine the chili powder, cumin, and cayenne in a small bowl then rub the mixture into the pork.
2. Place the pork in the Instant Pot, then pour in the water.
3. Close and lock the lid, then press the Manual button and adjust the timer to 40 minutes.
4. When the timer goes off, let the pressure vent for 15 minutes then do a Quick Release by pressing Cancel and switching the steam valve to "venting."
5. When the pot has depressurized, open the lid.
6. Shred the pork and season with salt and pepper then serve hot.

Nutrition:

calories 330 fat 8g ,protein 59.5g ,carbs 2g ,fiber 0.5g ,net carbs 1.5g

Ginger Soy-Glazed Pork Tenderloin

Prep Time + Cook time:15 minutes , Servings: 4

Ingredients:

- ¼ cup water
- 1 (1-pound) boneless pork tenderloin
- 1 tablespoon coconut flour

What you'll need from the store cupboard:

- Salt and pepper
- 2 tablespoons fresh grated ginger
- ½ cup soy sauce

Directions:

1. Whisk together the soy sauce, water, and ginger in a bowl.
2. Season the pork with salt and pepper then add to the Instant Pot.
3. Close and lock the lid then press the Manual button and adjust the timer to 5 minutes.
4. When the timer goes off, let the pressure vent for 10 minutes then do a Quick Release by pressing Cancel and switching the steam valve to "venting."
5. When the pot has depressurized, open the lid.
6. Remove the pork to a cutting board and cover with foil.
7. Stir the coconut flour into the cooking liquid then press the Sauté button.
8. Cook until thickened then slice the pork and pour the glaze over it to serve.

Nutrition:

calories 160 fat 4g ,protein 24g ,carbs 7.5g ,fiber 2g ,net carbs 5.5g

Herb-Roasted Lamb Shoulder

Prep Time + Cook time:50 minutes , Servings: 6

Ingredients:

- 1 ½ teaspoons fresh chopped rosemary
- 2 ½ pounds boneless lamb shoulder
- 1 cup water

What you'll need from the store cupboard:

- Salt and pepper
- 1 teaspoon fresh chopped oregano
- 1 tablespoon fresh chopped thyme

Directions:

1. Combine the herbs in a small bowl then rub it into the lamb and season with salt and pepper.
2. Place the lamb in the Instant Pot and add the water.
3. Close and lock the lid then press the Manual button and set the timer for 40 minutes.
4. When the timer goes off, let the pressure vent for 10 minutes then do a Quick Release by pressing Cancel and switching the steam valve to "venting."
5. When the pot has depressurized, open the lid.
6. Transfer the lamb to a roasting pan and broil for 10 minutes until browned.
7. Let the lamb rest on a cutting board for 10 minutes before slicing to serve.

Nutrition:

calories 360 fat 20g ,protein 42g ,carbs 1.5g ,fiber 0.5g ,net carbs 1g

Curried Pork Shoulder

Prep Time + Cook time:1 hour 5 minutes , Servings: 8

Ingredients:

- 4 pounds boneless pork shoulder, cut into large pieces
- 1 small yellow onion, chopped
- 3 ½ cups unsweetened coconut milk

What you'll need from the store cupboard:

- Salt and pepper
- 2 tablespoons olive oil
- 1 tablespoon fresh grated ginger
- 1 tablespoon curry powder

Directions:

1. Turn the Instant Pot on to the Sauté setting and let it heat up.
2. Add the olive oil to the pot and season the pork with salt and pepper.
3. Add the pork to the pot and cook until browned on all sides, about 8 minutes total.
4. Remove the pork to a cutting board then add the onions and ginger to the pot.
5. Cook for 3 minutes then add the coconut milk.
6. Add the pork back to the pot and sprinkle with curry powder.
7. Close and lock the lid then press the Manual button and cook on High Pressure for 55 minutes.
8. When the timer goes off, do a Quick Release by pressing Cancel and switching the steam valve to "venting."
9. When the pot has depressurized, open the lid.
10. Cut the pork into chunks and stir back into the sauce to serve.

Nutrition:

calories 380 fat 13.5g ,protein 59.5g ,carbs 2.5g ,fiber 1g ,net carbs 1.5g

Curried Lamb Stew

Prep Time + Cook time:1hour 5 minutes , Servings: 4

Ingredients:

- 1 small yellow onion, chopped
- 1 ½ pounds boneless lamb shoulder, chopped
- 2 cups chopped cauliflower
- 1 ½ cups chicken broth

What you'll need from the store cupboard:

- Salt and pepper
- 1 tablespoon olive oil
- 1 tablespoon curry powder

Directions:

1. Turn the Instant Pot on to the Sauté setting and let it heat up.
2. Add the oil then stir in the onions and cook for 4 minutes.
3. Stir in the chopped lamb, cauliflower, chicken broth, and curry powder. Season with salt and pepper.
4. Close and lock the lid, then press the Manual button and adjust the timer to 50 minutes.
5. When the timer goes off, let the pressure vent naturally.
6. When the pot has depressurized, open the lid.
7. Stir well and adjust seasonings to taste before serving.

Nutrition:

calories 385 fat 17g ,protein 51g ,carbs 5.5g ,fiber 2g ,net carbs 3.5g

Smothered Pork Chops

Prep Time + Cook time:40 minutes , Servings: 4

Ingredients:

- 4 (5-ounce) boneless pork loin chops
- 8 ounces sliced mushrooms

What you'll need from the store cupboard:

- Salt and pepper
- 2 tablespoons olive oil
- ½ cup heavy cream
- 1 tablespoon butter
- ½ teaspoon xanthan gum

Directions:

1. Turn the Instant Pot on to the Sauté setting and let it heat up.
2. Add the oil to the pot and season the pork chops with salt and pepper.
3. Place the pork chops in the pot and brown for 3 minutes on each side then remove to a plate.
4. Add the mushrooms to the pot and place the pork chops on top.
5. Close and lock the lid then press the Manual button and cook on High Pressure for 25 minutes.
6. When the timer goes off, let the pressure vent for 10 minutes then do a Quick Release by pressing Cancel and switching the steam valve to "venting."
7. When the pot has depressurized, open the lid.
8. Remove the pork chops to a plate then add the heavy cream and butter to the pot.
9. Sprinkle with xanthan gum, then simmer on the Sauté setting for 5 minutes until thickened.
10. Stir the gravy then spoon over the pork chops to serve.

Nutrition:

calories 350 fat 20.5g ,protein 39g ,carbs 2.5g ,fiber 0.5g ,net carbs 2g

Rosemary Garlic Leg of Lamb

Prep Time + Cook time:45 minutes , Servings: 8 to 10

Ingredients:

- 4 pounds boneless leg of lamb
- 2 tablespoons chopped rosemary
- 2 cups water

What you'll need from the store cupboard:

- Salt and pepper
- 2 tablespoons olive oil
- 1 tablespoon garlic

Directions:

1. Turn the Instant Pot on to the Sauté setting and let it heat up.
2. Add the oil then season the lamb with salt and pepper.
3. Place the lamb in the pot and cook for 2 to 3 minutes on each side to brown.
4. Remove the lamb and rub the garlic and rosemary into it.
5. Place the steamer insert in your pot and add the water.
6. Add the lamb to the steamer insert, then close and lock the lid.
7. Press the Meat/Stew button and adjust the timer to 30 minutes.
8. When the timer goes off, let the pressure vent naturally.
9. When the pot has depressurized, open the lid.
10. Let the lamb rest on a cutting board for 10 minutes before slicing.

Nutrition:

calories 365 fat 16g ,protein 51g ,carbs 1g ,fiber 0.5g ,net carbs 0.5g

Chapter 7 Soups and Stews Recipes

Hearty Beef and Bacon Chili

Prep Time + Cook time:40 minutes , Servings: 4

Ingredients:

- 6 slices bacon, chopped
- 2 small red peppers, chopped
- 1 pound ground beef (80% lean)
- 1 cup diced tomatoes

What you'll need from the store cupboard:

- Salt and pepper
- 1 teaspoon garlic powder
- 2 tablespoons chili powder
- 1 cup low-carb tomato sauce

Directions:

1. Turn on the Instant Pot to the Sauté setting and add the chopped bacon.
2. Let the bacon cook until it is crisp then remove it with a slotted spoon.
3. Add the red peppers to the pot.
4. Cook for 5 minutes, stirring, then add the rest of the ingredients.
5. Close and lock the lid, then press the Bean/Chili button to cook for 30 minutes.
6. When the timer goes off, let the pressure vent for 10 minutes then press Cancel to do a Quick Release by switching the steam valve to "venting."
7. Open the lid when the pot has depressurized and stir in the bacon.
8. Season with salt and pepper to taste then serve hot.

Nutrition:
calories 470 fat 30g ,protein 38g ,carbs 12g ,fiber 3.5g ,net carbs 8.5g

Clam and Cauliflower Chowder

Prep Time + Cook time:20 minutes , Servings: 6

Ingredients:

- 3 (6.5-ounce) cans chopped clams
- 1 small yellow onion
- 4 cups chopped cauliflower

What you'll need from the store cupboard:

- Salt and pepper
- 1 ½ cups heavy cream
- 3 tablespoons butter
- ½ teaspoon dried thyme
- Water

Directions:

1. Drain the clams into a bowl and add water to the juice to make 2 cups of liquid.
2. Turn the Instant Pot on to the Sauté setting then add the butter and onion.
3. Cook for 2 minutes, then add the cauliflower and clam juice.
4. Close and lock the lid, then push the Manual button and set the timer for 5 minutes.
5. When the timer goes off, let the pressure vent for 3 minutes, then press Cancel and do a Quick Release by switching the steam valve to "venting."
6. When the pot has depressurized, stir in the clams and heavy cream.
7. Cook on the Sauté setting until heated through then season with thyme, salt and pepper. Serve hot.

Nutrition:
calories 250 fat 17g ,protein 17g ,carbs 9g ,fiber 2g ,net carb 7g s

Buffalo Chicken Soup

Prep Time + Cook time:15 minutes , Servings: 6

Ingredients:

- ½ cup diced yellow onion
- 1 pound boneless chicken thighs, chopped (cooked)
- 4 cups chicken broth

What you'll need from the store cupboard:

- 1 tablespoon olive oil
- 6 ounces cream cheese, chopped
- 3 tablespoons hot sauce
- ½ cup heavy cream

Directions:

1. Turn the Instant Pot on to the Sauté setting and let it heat up.
2. Add the oil, then stir in the onion and cook for 3 to 4 minutes.
3. Stir in the chicken, chicken broth, and hot sauce.
4. Close and lock the lid, then press the Soup button and adjust the timer to 5 minutes.
5. When the timer goes off, let the pressure vent for 5 minutes, then do a Quick Release by pressing the Cancel button and switching the steam valve to "venting."
6. When the pot has depressurized, open the lid.
7. Spoon a cup of the soup into a blender and add the cream cheese.
8. Blend smooth then stir the mixture back into the pot with the heavy cream.
9. Stir until smooth then serve hot.

Nutrition:

calories 345 fat 28g ,protein 19g ,carbs 2.5g ,fiber 0g ,net carbs 2.5g

Cheesy Cauliflower Soup

Prep Time + Cook time:10 minutes , Servings: 4

Ingredients:

- 8 cups chopped cauliflower
- 3 cups chicken broth
- 4 ounces cream cheese, chopped
- 1 cup shredded cheddar cheese

What you'll need from the store cupboard:

- ½ cup heavy cream
- 2 tablespoons butter
- Salt and pepper to taste

Directions:

1. Turn the Instant Pot on to the Sauté setting and let it heat up.
2. Add the butter and cook for 30 seconds until melted.
3. Add the cauliflower and chicken broth, stirring to coat with butter.
4. Close and lock the lid, then press the Manual button and set the timer for 5 minutes on High Pressure.
5. When the timer goes off, press Cancel to do a Quick Release by switching the steam valve to "venting."
6. When the pot has depressurized, open the lid.
7. Puree the soup with an immersion blender then add the heavy cream, cream cheese, and cheddar cheese and stir until the cheese melts.
8. Adjust the seasoning to taste and serve hot.

Nutrition:

calories 395 fat 32g ,protein 17g ,carbs 13g ,fiber 5g ,net carbs 8g

Easy Taco Chicken Soup

Prep Time + Cook time:23 minutes , Servings: 4

Ingredients:

- 1 pound boneless chicken thighs, chopped
- ½ cup diced yellow onion
- 2 cups chicken broth
- 1 tablespoon chipotle chilis in adobo, chopped

What you'll need from the store cupboard:

- Salt and pepper
- 1 (8-ounce) package cream cheese, chopped
- 1 tablespoon ground cumin

Directions:

1. Turn the Instant Pot on to the Sauté setting and let it heat up.
2. Add the chicken and sauté for 3 minutes, stirring, until browned.
3. Stir in the rest of the ingredients aside from the cream cheese.
4. Close and lock the lid, then press the Manual button and adjust the timer to 18 minutes on High Pressure.
5. When the timer goes off, let the pressure vent for 10 minutes then press Cancel to do a Quick Release by switching the steam valve to "venting."
6. When the pot has depressurized, open the lid.
7. Stir in the cream cheese until it is melted and fully incorporated.
8. Season with salt and pepper, then serve with fresh cilantro, if desired.

Nutrition:

calories 470 fat 38g ,protein 27g ,carbs 4.5g ,fiber 1g ,net carbs 3.5g

Cauliflower And Beef Tomato Soup

Prep Time + Cook time: 35 minutes , Servings: 4

5-Ingredients:

- 1 tbsp Chopped cilantro
- 5 cups Chicken stock
- 2 Chopped shallots
- 15 oz Chopped canned tomatoes
- 1 Lb. Cubed beef stew meat

What you'll need from the store cupboard:

- A pinch of salt and black pepper
- 1 tbsp Olive oil

Directions:

1. Press 'Sauté' on the instant pot and add the oil. When it is hot, brown the beef stew meat and the shallot for 5 minutes.
2. Mix in the cilantro, chicken stock, tomatoes, salt, and pepper and seal the lid to cook for 20 minutes at high pressure.
3. Natural release the pressure for 10 minutes, share into bowls and serve.

Nutrition

Calories 272, fat 11.5, carbs 5.1, protein 35.6, fiber 1.3

Instant Pot Brussels Sprouts And Chicken Soup

Prep Time + Cook time: 35 minutes , Servings: 4

5-Ingredients:

- 1 ½ cups Chicken stock
- 2 Chopped scallions
- ½ Lb. Halved Brussels sprouts
- 1 Lb. Cubed skinless and boneless chicken breasts .

What you'll need from the store cupboard:

- A pinch of salt and black pepper

- 1 tbsp Avocado oil
- 1 tbsp Tomato paste
- 1 tsp Chopped basil

Directions:
1. Press 'Sauté' on the instant pot and add the avocado oil. When it is hot, mix in the chicken and scallions to brown for 5 minutes.

2. Add the tomato paste, salt and pepper, chicken stock, basil, and Brussels sprouts to the pot and seal the lid to cook for 20 minutes at high pressure.
3. Natural release the pressure for 10 minutes, share into bowls and serve.

Nutrition
Calories 250, fat 9.1, carbs 6.7, protein 35.1, fiber 2.7

Seafood in Tomato Soup

Prep Time + Cook time: 19 minutes , Servings: 4

5-Ingredients:
- 1 ½ lb. Shrimp; peeled and deveined
- 2 cups Veggie stock
- 2 tbsp Chopped parsley
- 20 oz Chopped canned tomatoes
- 1 ½ lbs. Cubed boneless and skinless cod fillets

What you'll need from the store cupboard:
- A pinch of salt and black pepper
- 3 cloves Minced garlic

- 1 tbsp Dried basil

Directions:
1. Mix all the ingredients in the instant pot and seal the lid to cook for 14 minutes at high pressure.
2. Quick-release the pressure for 5 minutes, share into bowls and serve.

Nutrition
Calories 130, fat 7.5, carbs 6.4, protein 1.5, fiber 1.8

Creamy Lime Artichokes

Prep Time + Cook time: 25 minutes , Servings: 4

5-Ingredients:
- 2 cups Chopped artichoke hearts
- 6 cups Chicken stock
- 1 Chopped shallot
- ½ cup Coconut cream
- 3 tbsp Ghee

What you'll need from the store cupboard:
- A pinch of salt and black pepper
- ¼ tsp Lime juice .
- 1 tsp Dried rosemary

Directions:

1. Press 'Sauté' on the instant pot and add the ghee to melt then mix in the shallot to cook for 2 minutes.
2. Mix in the remaining ingredients and seal the lid to cook for 13 minutes at high pressure.
3. Natural release the pressure for 10 minutes and puree the soup with a dipping blender, dish into bowls and serve.

Nutrition
Calories 169, fat 17.6, carbs 3, protein 1.8, fiber 0.3

Tomato Leek Soup

Prep Time + Cook time: 25 minutes , Servings: 4

5-Ingredients:
- 1 tbsp Chopped cilantro
- 4 cups Chicken stock
- 2 Chopped leeks
- 1 Minced shallot

What you'll need from the store cupboard:
- A pinch of salt and black pepper
- 1 tbsp Olive oil .
- 1 tbsp Sweet paprika
- 1 tbsp Tomato paste

Directions:

1. Press 'Sauté' on the instant pot and add the olive oil. When hot, mix in the minced shallot and the leeks to cook for 2 minutes.
2. Mix in the remaining ingredients and seal the lid to cook for 13 minutes at high pressure.
3. Natural release the pressure for 10 minutes, dish into bowls and serve.

Nutrition
Calories 75, fat 4.4, carbs 3.4, protein 1.8, fiber 1.6

Kale And Bell Peppers In Tomato Soup

Prep Time + Cook time: 25 minutes , Servings: 4

5-Ingredients:
- 1 tbsp Chopped cilantro
- 4 cups Chicken stock
- ½ lb. Torn kale
- 4 Deseeded and roughly chopped red bell peppers

What you'll need from the store cupboard:
- A pinch of salt and black pepper
- 1 cup Tomato passata

Directions:
1. Mix all the ingredients in the instant pot and seal the lid to cook for 15 minutes at high pressure.
2. Natural release the pressure for 10 minutes, share into bowls and serve.

Nutrition
Calories 100, fat 6.3, carbs 3.7, protein 21.2, fiber 2.2

Herb Olives and Tomatoes Stew

Prep Time + Cook time: 20 minutes , Servings: 4

5-Ingredients:
- 1 lb. Cubed tomatoes
- 1 cup Chicken stock
- 1 cup Pitted Kalamata olives

What you'll need from the store cupboard:
- A pinch of salt and black pepper
- 1 tbsp Olive oil
- 1 tsp Dried thyme
- 1 tbsp Chopped oregano

Directions:

1. Press 'Sauté' on the instant pot and add the oil. When hot, pour in the tomatoes to cook for 2 minutes.
2. Mix in the olives, thyme, chicken stock, salt, and pepper and seal the lid to cook for 15 minutes at high pressure.
3. Quick-release the pressure, mix in the oregano, share into bowls and serve.

Nutrition
Calories 96, fat 7.6, carbs 6.8, protein 1.6, fiber 3

Garlic Cabbage and Tomatoes Soup

Prep Time + Cook time: 30 minutes , Servings: 4

5-Ingredients:
- 14 oz Chopped canned tomatoes
- 1 Chopped celery stalk
- 1 cup Veggie stock
- 2 cups Shredded green cabbage
- 1 tsp Turmeric powder

What you'll need from the store cupboard:
- A pinch of salt and black pepper
- ½ tbsp Avocado oil
- 3 cloves Chopped garlic

Directions:

1. Press 'Sauté' on the instant pot and add the oil. When it is hot, mix in the garlic and the celery to cook for 2 minutes.
2. Mix in the remaining ingredients, then seal the lid to cook for 15 minutes at high pressure.
3. Natural release the pressure for 10 minutes, share into bowls and serve.

Nutrition
Calories 35, fat 4.2, carbs 3.2, protein 1.6, fiber 2.4

Her By Zucchini And Broccoli Soup

Prep Time + Cook time: 25 minutes , Servings: 4

5-Ingredients:
- 1 tbsp Chopped cilantro
- 4 cups Chicken stock
- 1 Chopped shallot
- 1 lb. Sliced zucchini
- 1 lb. Broccoli florets

What you'll need from the store cupboard:
- 2 tsp Avocado oil
- 1 tsp Dried basil

Directions:

1. Press 'Sauté' on the instant pot and add the oil. When it is hot, fry the shallot for 2 minutes.
2. Mix in the zucchini, broccoli, and the remaining ingredients then seal the lid to cook for 12 minutes at high pressure.
3. Natural release the pressure for 10 minutes, scoop into soup bowls and serve.

Nutrition
Calories 70, fat 11.3, carbs 6.7, protein 5.3, fiber 4.3

Spicy Beef with Chives

Prep Time + Cook time: 35 minutes , Servings: 4

5-Ingredients:
- 1 ½ lbs. Cubed beef
- 1 tbsp Chopped parsley
- 6 cups Veggie stock
- 1 cup Chopped scallions
- 1 tbsp Sweet paprika

What you'll need from the store cupboard:
- A pinch of salt and black pepper
- 2 tbsp Olive oil

Directions:

1. Press 'Sauté' on the instant pot and add the oil. When hot, brown the scallions and the beef for 5 minutes.
2. Mix in the remaining ingredients, seal the lid and cook for 20 minutes at high pressure.
3. Natural release the pressure for 10 minutes, then dish into bowls and serve.

Nutrition
Calories 73, fat 7.3, carbs 2.9, protein 0.8, fiber 1.3

Creamy Garlic Tomato Soup

Prep Time + Cook time: 30 minutes , Servings: 4

5-Ingredients:
- 2 tbsp Chopped chives
- 2 cups Chicken stock
- 1 lb. Tomatoes; peeled and chopped
- 1 tbsp Chopped cilantro
- 2 cups Coconut cream

What you'll need from the store cupboard:
- A pinch of salt and black pepper
- 1 tbsp Red curry paste
- 3 cloves Minced garlic

Directions:
1. Pour the stock into the instant pot and add the salt, pepper, garlic, and chopped tomatoes then seal the lid to cook for 20 minutes at high pressure.
2. Natural release the pressure for 10 minutes and pour the contents into a blender, then add the curry paste and the coconut cream and blend until smooth. Share into bowls and serve topped with cilantro and chives.

Nutrition
Calories 320, fat 30.2, carbs 8.1, protein 4.2, fiber 4.1

Veggie Soup

Prep Time + Cook time: 21 minutes , Servings: 4

5-Ingredients:
- 2 tbsp Chopped dill
- 1 Chopped shallot
- 1 lb. Shredded green cabbage
- 12 cups Chicken stock
- 1 Chopped celery stalk

What you'll need from the store cupboard:
- A pinch of salt and black pepper
- 1 tbsp Olive oil

Directions:
1. Press 'Sauté' on the instant pot and add the olive oil. When it is hot, mix in the shallot to reduce for 2 minutes.
2. Add the dill, green cabbage, chicken stock, celery stalk, salt, and black pepper then seal the lid to cook for 13 minutes at high pressure.
3. Quick-release the pressure for 6 minutes, scoop into bowls and serve.

Nutrition
Calories 92, fat 5.4, carbs 5.7, protein 3.9, fiber 3.1

Cheesy Creamy Soup

Prep Time + Cook time: 25 minutes , Servings: 4

5-Ingredients:
- 1 cup Grated cheddar cheese
- 2 tbsp Chopped parsley
- ½ cup Chopped spring onions
- 6 cups Chicken stock
- 2 cups Coconut cream

What you'll need from the store cupboard:
- A pinch of salt and black pepper
- 2 tbsp Olive oil

Directions:
1. Press 'Sauté' on the instant pot and add the oil. When it is hot, add the spring onions to cook for 2-3 minutes.

2. Whisk in the rest of the ingredients, seal the lid and cook for 15 minutes at high pressure.
3. Natural release the pressure for 10 minutes, share into bowls and serve.

Nutrition
Calories 313, fat 30.5, carbs 6.1, protein 7.4, fiber 2

Eggplant, Tomatoes and Celery Soup

Prep Time + Cook time: 25 minutes , Servings: 4

5-Ingredients:
- 8 cups Chicken stock
- 1 Chopped celery stalk
- 2 Chopped tomatoes
- 3 Cubed eggplants
- 1 Chopped shallot

What you'll need from the store cupboard:
- 1 tbsp Avocado oil
- A pinch of salt and pepper
- 2 tbsp Chopped rosemary

Directions:

1. Press 'Sauté' on the instant pot and add the oil. When hot, add the celery and shallot to cook for 3 minutes.
2. Mix in the remaining ingredients, then seal the lid to cook for 12 minutes at high pressure.
3. Natural release the pressure for 10 minutes, dish into bowls and serve.

Nutrition
Calories 144, fat 5.7, carbs 5.3, protein 6.1, fiber 0.2

Creamy Red Bell Pepper and Tomato Soup

Prep Time + Cook time: 30 minutes , Servings: 4

5-Ingredients:
- 1 tsp Chopped chives
- 1 Chopped shallot
- 6 cups Chicken stock
- 4 Red bell peppers; chopped roughly
- 2 Cubed tomatoes

What you'll need from the store cupboard:
- 2 tbsp Olive oil
- 3 tbsp Tomato paste
- ½ tsp Red pepper flakes

Directions:
1. Press 'Sauté' on the instant pot and pour in the olive oil. When it is hot, add in the shallot to cook for 2 minutes.

2. Add the red bell peppers, tomatoes, tomato paste, chicken stock, and red pepper flakes and mix then seal the lid to cook for 18 minutes at high pressure.
3. Natural release the pressure for 10 minutes and puree the soup with a blender, share it into bowls and serve with chives.

Nutrition
Calories 134, fat 8.4, carbs 5.4, protein 3.3, fiber 2.8

Chili Chicken with Asparagus Soup

Prep Time + Cook time: 30 minutes , Servings: 4

5-Ingredients:

- 5 cups Chicken stock
- ¼ cup Chopped parsley
- 1 Asparagus stalk; trimmed and halved
- 2 Chicken breasts; skinless and boneless; cubed
- 2 Chopped scallions

What you'll need from the store cupboard:

- A pinch of salt and black pepper
- 1 tbsp Avocado oil
- 1 tbsp Sweet chili sauce

Directions:

1. Press 'Sauté' on the instant pot then add the oil. When hot, mix in the chili sauce and scallions to cook for 3 minutes.
2. Add the chicken to brown for 2 minutes.
3. Mix in the remaining ingredients, then seal the lid to cook for 15 minutes at high pressure.
4. Natural release the pressure for 10 minutes, share into bowls and serve.

Nutrition

Calories 108, fat 4.4, carbs 3.1, protein 1.1, fiber 0.5

Ginger Chicken and Mushroom Soup

Prep Time + Cook time: 30 minutes , Servings: 4

5-Ingredients:

- 1 lb. Chicken breast; skinless and boneless; cubed .
- 1 Chopped shallot
- 1 quart Chicken stock
- 1 lb. Sliced mushrooms

What you'll need from the store cupboard:

- A pinch of salt and black pepper
- 1 tbsp Olive oil
- 2 tsp Minced ginger

Directions:

1. Press 'Sauté' on the instant pot and add the oil. When it is hot, mix in the mushrooms and shallot to fry for 4 minutes.
2. Mix in the remaining ingredients, then seal the lid to cook for 15 minutes at high pressure.
3. Natural release the pressure for 10 minutes, share into bowls and serve.

Nutrition

Calories 203, fat 7.4, carbs 6.4, protein 28.5, fiber 1.5

Cheesy Okra Soup

Prep Time + Cook time: 25 minutes , Servings: 4

5-Ingredients:

- ½ cup Coconut milk
- 1 cup Shredded cheddar cheese
- 1 Chopped spring onion
- 3 cups Okra
- 3 cups Chicken stock

What you'll need from the store cupboard:

- 2 tbsp Olive oil
- 1 tsp Garlic powder
- A pinch of salt and pepper

Directions:

1. Press 'Sauté' on the instant pot and add the oil. When hot, mix in the onion to cook for 2 minutes.
2. Mix in the remaining ingredients and seal the lid to cook for 13 minutes at high pressure.
3. Natural release the pressure for 10 minutes, share into bowls and serve.

Nutrition

Calories 284, fat 24.1, carbs 7, protein 9.9, fiber 3.2

Pork Soup Topped with Chives

Prep Time + Cook time: 35 minutes , Servings: 4

5-Ingredients:

- 1 tbsp Chopped chives
- 15 oz Chopped tomatoes
- 1 ½ lbs. Cubed pork stew meat
- 8 cups Chicken stock

What you'll need from the store cupboard:

- A pinch of salt and black pepper

Directions:

1. Combine all the ingredients in the instant pot, saving the chives to top when serving and seal the lid to cook for 25 minutes at high pressure.
2. Natural release the pressure for 10 minutes and share into bowls, then sprinkle the chives over it and serve.

Nutrition

Calories 39, fat 4.3, carbs 3.4, protein 2.4, fiber 1.2

Chapter 8 Vegetable recipes

Cheesy Broccoli With Chives

Prep Time + Cook time: 25 minutes , Servings: 4

5-Ingredients:

- 2 cups Shredded cheddar cheese
- 1 Broccoli head; florets separated
- 1 tbsp Chopped chives
- 4 cups Chicken stock
- 1 cup Coconut cream

What you'll need from the store cupboard:

- ¼ tsp Garlic powder
- A pinch of salt and white pepper

Directions:

1. Mix the chives, stock, broccoli florets, salt, and white pepper, and garlic powder in the instant pot, seal the lid to cook for 10 minutes at high pressure.
2. Natural release the pressure for 10 minutes and change the pot setting to 'Sauté.' Mix in the cream and cheese and blend with a dipping blender then let it cook for 5 minutes.
3. Share into bowls and serve.

Nutrition

Calories 376, fat 33.5, carbs 4.9, protein 16.2, fiber 1.4

Brussels Sprouts Cream

Prep Time + Cook time: 30 minutes , Servings: 4

5-Ingredients:

- 1 tbsp Chopped chives
- 1 cup Chicken stock
- 2 Chopped shallots
- 1 lb. Halved Brussels sprouts
- 1 cup Coconut cream

What you'll need from the store cupboard:

- A pinch of salt and black pepper
- 1 tbsp Olive oil

Directions:

1. Press 'Sauté' on the instant pot and add the olive oil. When it is hot, reduce the shallots in the oil for 5 minutes.
2. Mix in the cream, stock, Brussels sprouts, salt, and pepper then seal the lid to cook for 20 minutes at high pressure.
3. Quick-release the pressure for 5 minutes, sprinkle the chives into the mix and stir the stew, share into bowls and serve.

Nutrition

Calories 220, fat 16.7, carbs 6.8, protein 5.4, fiber 5.6

Nutmeg Spiced Endives

Prep time + Cook time: 20 minutes , Servings: 4

5-Ingredients:

- 4 (trimmed and halved) Endives
- 1 cup Water
- 1 tsp (ground) Nutmeg
- 1 tbsp (chopped) Chives

What you'll need from the store cupboard:

- 2 tbsp Olive oil
- Salt and black pepper to the taste

Directions:

1. Pour water into the Instant Pot and place the steamer basket over it.
2. Place endives in this steamer basket.
3. Seal the pot's lid and cook for 10 minutes on manual mode at High.
4. Allow the pressure to release in 10 minutes naturally then remove the lid.
5. Toss them with salt, pepper, nutmeg, oil and chives.
6. Serve fresh and enjoy.

Nutrition:
Calories 63, Total Fat: 7.2g, Carbs: 0.3g, Protein: 0.1g, Fiber: 0.1g.

Cabbage Radish Medley

Prep time + Cook time: 25 minutes , Servings: 4

5-Ingredients:
- 1 (shredded) Red cabbage head
- 2 tbsp Veggie stock
- 1 cup (sliced) Radish
- 1 tbsp Coconut aminos
- ½ inch (grated) Ginger

What you'll need from the store cupboard:
- 1 tbsp Olive oil
- 3 (minced) Garlic cloves

Directions:
1. Let your Instant Pot preheat on Sauté mode.
2. Add oil, ginger, and garlic to the pot.
3. Sauté for 3 minutes, then stir in remaining ingredients.
4. Seal the lid pot's lid and cook for 12 minutes on manual high settings.
5. Allow the pressure to release naturally in 10 minutes.
6. Serve warm and fresh.

Nutrition:
Calories 83, Total Fat: 4.4g, Carbs: 3.3g, Protein: 2.6g, Fiber: 2.1g.

Saucy Passata Brussels Sprouts

Prep time + Cook time: 20 minutes , Servings: 4

5-Ingredients:
- 1 pound (halved) Brussels sprouts
- ¼ cup Chicken stock
- 1 tbsp (chopped) Green onions
- 1 tbsp (chopped) Chives
- 1 cup Tomato passata

What you'll need from the store cupboard:
- 2 tbsp Olive oil
- a pinch Salt and black pepper

Directions:
1. Add sprouts, stock, salt, black pepper, passata, chives, olive oil and green onions to the Instant Pot.
2. Seal the lid of the pot and cook for 10 minutes on Manual mode at High.
3. Allow the pressure to release naturally in 10 minutes.
4. Serve fresh.

Nutrition:
Calories 112, Total Fat: 7.5g, Carbs: 4.5g, Protein: 4g, Fiber: 2.4g.

Cheesy Broccoli Bites

Prep time + Cook time: 20 minutes , Servings: 4

5-Ingredients:
- 1 pound Broccoli florets
- ½ cup Veggie stock
- 2 (chopped) Shallots
- 1 cup (shredded) Mozzarella cheese
- 1 tbsp (chopped) Cilantro

What you'll need from the store cupboard:
- 3 tbsp Olive oil
- Salt and black pepper

Directions:
1. Let your Instant pot preheat on Sauté mode.
2. Add oil and shallots to the pot and stir cook for 2 minutes.
3. Stir in remaining ingredients except for the mozzarella cheese.
4. Mix well then top the mixture with mozzarella cheese.
5. Seal the lid of the pot and cook for 8 minutes on manual mode at High.
6. Allow the pressure to release naturally for 10 minutes.
7. Serve fresh and enjoy.

Nutrition:
Calories 149, Total Fat: 12.1g, Carbs: 7.8g, Protein: 5.2g, Fiber: 3g.

Balsamic Mushrooms

Prep time + Cook time: 25 minutes , Servings: 4

5-Ingredients:
- 1 pound (sliced) White mushrooms
- ¼ cup Chicken stock
- 1 cup (sliced) Radishes
- 1 tbsp (chopped) Parsley

What you'll need from the store cupboard:
- 2 tbsp Avocado oil
- 2 tbsp Balsamic vinegar
- a pinch Salt and black pepper

Directions:
1. Let your Instant Pot preheat on Sauté mode.
2. Add oil and mushrooms to sauté for 5 minutes.
3. Stir in remaining ingredients and mix well
4. Seal the pot's lid and cook for 10 minutes on manual mode at High.
5. Allow the pressure to release in 10 minutes then remove the lid.
6. Serve fresh and enjoy.

Nutrition:
Calories 41, Total Fat: 4.3g, Carbs: 3.5g, Protein: 3.9g, Fiber: 1.9g.

Balsamic Glazed Spinach

Prep time + Cook time: 12 minutes , Servings: 4

5-Ingredients:
- ¼ cup Veggie stock
- 1 and ½ pound Baby spinach
- 1 tbsp (chopped) Walnuts
- 1 tbsp (chopped) Chives

What you'll need from the store cupboard:
- 1 tbsp Balsamic vinegar

Directions:
1. Add spinach along with all the ingredients to the Instant Pot.

2. Seal the pot's lid and cook for 7 minutes on manual mode at High.
3. Allow the pressure to release in 5 minutes then remove the lid.
4. Serve fresh and enjoy.

Nutrition:
Calories 13, Total Fat: 1.2g, Carbs: 0.3g, Protein: 0.5g, Fiber: 0.2g.

Tangy White Mushrooms

Prep time + Cook time: 25minutes , Servings: 4
5-Ingredients:
- 1 and ½ pound (sliced) White mushrooms
- 1 cup Veggie stock
- 1 tbsp (chopped) Dill
- 1 tbsp (chopped) Rosemary

What you'll need from the store cupboard:
- 1 tbsp Avocado oil
- 1 tbsp Sweet paprika
- a pinch Salt and black pepper

Directions:
1. Let your Instant Pot preheat on Sauté mode.
2. Add oil and mushrooms, to sauté for 5 minutes.
3. Stir in remaining ingredients and mix well
4. Seal the pot's lid and cook for 10 minutes on manual mode at High.
5. Allow the pressure to release in 10 minutes then remove the lid.
6. Serve fresh and enjoy.

Nutrition:
Calories 14, Total Fat: 2.3g, Carbs: 2.1g, Protein: 0.5g, Fiber: 1.3g.

Creamy Coconut Spinach

Prep time + Cook time: 12 minutes , Servings: 4
5-Ingredients:
- 1 and ½ lbs. Baby spinach
- 1 tbsp (chopped) Cilantro
- ¼ cup Coconut cream

What you'll need from the store cupboard:
- 1 tbsp Chili powder
- Salt and black pepper

Directions:
1. Add spinach along with all the remaining ingredients to the Instant Pot.
2. Seal the pot's lid and cook for 7 minutes on manual mode at High.
3. Allow the pressure to release in 5 minutes then remove the lid.
4. Serve fresh and enjoy.

Nutrition:
Calories 41, Total Fat: 3.9g, Carbs: 1.9g, Protein: 0.6g, Fiber: 1g.

Chili Eggplant Luncheon

Prep time + Cook time: 25 minutes , Servings: 4
5-Ingredients:
- 1 big (cubed) Eggplant
- 1 pound (halved) Collard greens
- ½ cup Chicken stock
- 1 tbsp (chopped) Cilantro
- 4 (chopped) Green onions

What you'll need from the store cupboard:
- 2 tbsp Avocado oil
- 2 tsp Chili paste

Directions:

82

1. Let your Instant Pot preheat on Sauté mode.
2. Add oil, eggplants, and spring onions to sauté for 4 minutes.
3. Stir in remaining ingredients and mix well.
4. Seal the pot's lid and cook for 10 minutes on manual mode at High.
5. Allow the pressure to release in 10 minutes then remove the lid.
6. Serve fresh and enjoy.

Nutrition:
Calories 84, Total Fat: 2.4g, Carbs: 6g, Protein: 4.2g, Fiber: 2g.

Easy Italian Asparagus

Prep time + Cook time: 8 minutes , Servings: 4

5-Ingredients:
- 1 cup Water
- 1 pound (trimmed) Asparagus
- 1 tbsp (chopped) Cilantro
- 1 tbsp Lemon juice

What you'll need from the store cupboard:
- 1 tsp Olive oil
- ½ tbsp Italian seasoning
- a pinch Salt and black pepper

Directions:
1. Pour water into the Instant Pot and place steamer basket over it.
2. Place asparagus in the steamer basket.
3. Seal the pot's lid and cook for 4 minutes on manual mode at High.
4. Allow the pressure to release in 4 minutes naturally then remove the lid.
5. Toss the asparagus with all other ingredients in a platter.
6. Serve fresh and enjoy.

Nutrition:
Calories 39, Total Fat: 2.1g, Carbs: 1.3g, Protein: 2.5g, Fiber: 1.1g.

White Mushrooms and Chard Mix

Prep time + Cook time: 22 minutes , Servings: 4

5-Ingredients:
- 1 pound (sliced) White mushrooms
- 1 red (roughly chopped) Chard bunch
- ¼ cup Chicken stock
- 3 tbsp (chopped) Parsley

What you'll need from the store cupboard:
- 2 tbsp Olive oil
- 1 tsp Garlic powder
- a pinch Salt and black pepper

Directions:
1. Let your Instant Pot preheat on Sauté mode.
2. Add oil and mushrooms to sauté for 2 minutes.
3. Stir in remaining ingredients and mix well.
4. Seal the pot's lid and cook for 10 minutes on manual mode at High.
5. Allow the pressure to release in 10 minutes then remove the lid.
6. Serve fresh and enjoy.

Nutrition:
Calories 88, Total Fat: 7.4g, Carbs: 4.5g, Protein: 3.8g, Fiber: 1.3g.

Creamy Coconut Cauliflower

Prep time + Cook time: 25 minutes , Servings: 4

5-Ingredients:
- 1 pound Cauliflower florets
- 1 cup (chopped) Red onion
- ¼ cup Chicken stock
- 1 cup Coconut cream

What you'll need from the store cupboard:
- 2 tbsp Balsamic vinegar
- a pinch Salt and black pepper

Directions:

1. Add cauliflower along with remaining ingredients to the Instant Pot.
2. Seal the pot's lid and cook for 15 minutes on manual mode at High.
3. Allow the pressure to release in 10 minutes then remove the lid.
4. Serve fresh and enjoy.

Nutrition:
Calories 180, Total Fat: 14.5g, Carbs: 7.5g, Protein: 4g, Fiber: 4.5g.

Parmesan cream Green Beans

Prep time + Cook time: 25 minutes , Servings: 4

5-Ingredients:
- 10 oz. (trimmed and halved) Green beans
- 1/3 cup (grated) Parmesan
- 2 oz Cream cheese
- 1 tbsp (chopped) Dill
- 1/3 cup Coconut cream

What you'll need from the store cupboard:
- A pinch Salt and black pepper

Directions:

1. Add green beans, cream cheese and all the ingredients to the Instant Pot.
2. Seal the pot's lid and cook for 15 minutes on manual mode at High.
3. Allow the pressure to release in 10 minutes then remove the lid.
4. Serve fresh and enjoy.

Nutrition:
Calories 119, Total Fat: 9.8g, Carbs: 6g, Protein: 3g, Fiber: 3g.

Radish Spinach Medley

Prep time + Cook time: 12 minutes , Servings: 4

5-Ingredients:
- 1 pound (torn) Spinach
- 2 cups (sliced) Radishes
- ¼ cup Veggie stock
- 1 tbsp (chopped) Parsley

What you'll need from the store cupboard:
- 1 tsp Chili powder
- a pinch Salt and black pepper

Directions:

1. Add spinach, radishes along with remaining ingredients to an Instant Pot.
2. Seal the pot's lid and cook for 7 minutes on manual mode at High.
3. Allow the pressure to release in 5 minutes then remove the lid.
4. Serve fresh and enjoy.

Nutrition:
Calories 70, Total Fat: 4.4g, Carbs: 4g, Protein: 3.7g, Fiber: 3.7g.

Citrus rich Cabbage

Prep time + Cook time: 20 minutes , Servings: 4

5-Ingredients:
- 1 pound (shredded) Green cabbage
- ½ cup Chicken stock
- 1 tbsp (chopped) Chives
- 1 tbsp Lemon juice
- 1 tbsp (grated) Lemon zest

What you'll need from the store cupboard:
- a pinch Salt and black pepper

Directions:

1. Add cabbage, stock and remaining ingredients to an Instant Pot.
2. Seal the pot's lid and cook for 10 minutes on manual mode at High.
3. Allow the pressure to release in 10 minutes then remove the lid.
4. Serve fresh and enjoy.

Nutrition:
Calories 34, Total Fat: 2.4g, Carbs: 1.9g, Protein: 1.6g, Fiber: 1g.

Creamy Mustard Asparagus

Prep time + Cook time: 13 minutes , Servings: 4

5-Ingredients:
- 1 pound (trimmed and halved) Asparagus
- 1 tbsp (chopped) Chives
- ¼ cup Coconut cream

What you'll need from the store cupboard:
- Salt and black pepper to the taste
- 2 tsp Mustard
- 2 (minced) Garlic cloves

Directions:

1. Add asparagus along with remaining ingredients to the Instant Pot.
2. Seal the pot's lid and cook for 8 minutes on manual mode at High.
3. Allow the pressure to release in 5 minutes naturally then remove the lid.
4. Serve fresh and enjoy.

Nutrition:
Calories 67, Total Fat: 4.2g, Carbs: 3.9g, Protein: 3.4g, Fiber: 3g.

Savory Pine Nuts Cabbage

Prep time + Cook time: 25 minutes , Servings: 4

5-Ingredients:
- 1 (shredded) Savoy cabbage
- ¼ cup Pine nuts, toasted
- ½ cup Veggie stock

What you'll need from the store cupboard:
- 2 tbsp Avocado oil
- 1 tbsp Balsamic vinegar
- Salt and black pepper to the taste

Directions:

1. Let your Instant Pot preheat on Sauté mode.
2. Add oil and cabbage, to sauté for 2 minutes.
3. Stir in remaining ingredients and mix well
4. Seal the pot's lid and cook for 15 minutes on manual mode at High.
5. Allow the pressure to release in 10 minutes naturally then remove the lid.
6. Serve fresh and enjoy.

Nutrition:
Calories 67, Total Fat: 6.7g, Carbs: 1.5g, Protein: 1.3g, Fiber: 0.5g.

Nutmeg Fennel

Prep time + Cook time: 20 minutes , Servings: 4

5-Ingredients:
- 2 (sliced) Fennel bulbs
- 2 and ½ cups Baby spinach
- ½ tsp (ground) Nutmeg
- ¼ cup Veggie stock

What you'll need from the store cupboard:
- 2 tbsp Balsamic vinegar
- 2 tbsp Olive oil
- 4 (chopped) Garlic cloves

Directions:

1. Add spinach and fennel along with all the ingredients to your Instant Pot.
2. Seal the pot's lid and cook for 10 minutes on manual mode at High.
3. Allow the pressure to release in 10 minutes naturally then remove the lid.
4. Serve fresh and enjoy.

Nutrition:
Calories 104, Total Fat: 7.4g, Carbs: 6.4g, Protein: 1.7g, Fiber: 3.6g.

Herbed Cherry Tomatoes

Prep time + Cook time: 22 minutes , Servings: 4

5-Ingredients:
- 2 lbs. (halved) Cherry tomatoes
- 1 tbsp (chopped) Dill
- ½ cups Chicken stock
- ¼ cup (chopped) Basil

What you'll need from the store cupboard:
- 2 tbsp Olive oil
- a pinch Salt and black pepper
- 4 (minced) Garlic cloves

Directions:
1. Let your Instant Pot preheat on Sauté mode.
2. Add oil and garlic, to sauté for 2 minutes.
3. Stir in remaining ingredients and mix well
4. Seal the pot's lid and cook for 10 minutes on manual mode at High.
5. Allow the pressure to release in 10 minutes naturally then remove the lid.
6. Serve fresh and enjoy.

Nutrition:
Calories 109, Total Fat: 7.6g, Carbs: 6.8g, Protein: 2.5g, Fiber: 2.9g.

Spicy Rosemary Cauliflower

Prep time + Cook time: 22 minutes , Servings: 4

5-Ingredients:
- 1 pound Cauliflower florets
- 1 cup Chicken stock
- 1 tbsp (chopped) Rosemary
- 2 (minced) Garlic cloves

What you'll need from the store cupboard:
- 1 tsp Hot chili sauce
- a pinch Salt and black pepper

Directions:

1. Add cauliflower, stock and all the ingredients to the Instant Pot.
2. Seal the pot's lid and cook for 12 minutes on manual mode at High.
3. Allow the pressure to release in 10 minutes naturally then remove the lid.
4. Serve fresh and enjoy.

Nutrition:
Calories 36, Total Fat: 2.4g, Carbs: 2.3g, Protein: 3.6g, Fiber: 1.5g.

Rich Creamy Endives

Prep time + Cook time: 20 minutes , Servings: 4

5-Ingredients:

- 4 (trimmed and halved) Endives
- ½ cup Chicken stock
- 1 tbsp (chopped) Dill
- ¼ cup Coconut cream

What you'll need from the store cupboard:

- 1 tbsp Smoked paprika

Directions:

1. Add endives along with remaining ingredients to the Instant Pot
2. Seal the pot's lid and cook for 10 minutes on manual mode at High.
3. Allow the pressure to release in 10 minutes naturally then remove the lid.
4. Serve fresh and enjoy.

Nutrition:

Calories 43, Total Fat: 3.9g, Carbs: 2.3g, Protein: 0.9g, Fiber: 1.1g.

Celery and Broccoli Medley

Prep time + Cook time: 22 minutes , Servings: 4

5-Ingredients:

- 1 and ½ cups Broccoli florets
- 1 (chopped) Celery stalk
- ½ cups Veggie stock
- 2 tbsp Lime juice
- 2 (minced) Garlic cloves

What you'll need from the store cupboard:

- 1 tbsp Olive oil
- a pinch Salt and black pepper

Directions:

1. Let your Instant Pot preheat on Sauté mode.
2. Add oil, garlic, and celery, to sauté for 2 minutes.
3. Stir in remaining ingredients and mix well.
4. Seal the pot's lid and cook for 10 minutes on manual mode at High.
5. Allow the pressure to release in 10 minutes naturally then remove the lid.
6. Serve fresh and enjoy.

Nutrition:

Calories 33, Total Fat: 3.5g, Carbs: 0.7g, Protein: 0.1g, Fiber: 0.1g.

Mediterranean Cauliflower Rice

Prep time + Cook time: 25 minutes , Servings: 4

5-Ingredients:

- 1 cup Cauliflower rice
- 1 and ½ cup Chicken stock
- 1 cup (pitted and sliced) Black olives
- 1 tbsp (chopped) Chives
- ½ cup (chopped) Cilantro

What you'll need from the store cupboard:

- A pinch Salt and black pepper

Directions:

1. Toss cauliflower rice and all the ingredients into the Instant Pot.
2. Seal the pot's lid and cook for 15 minutes on manual mode at High.
3. Allow the pressure to release in 10 minutes naturally then remove the lid.
4. Serve fresh and enjoy.

Nutrition:

Calories 40, Total Fat: 3.6g, Carbs: 2.2g, Protein: 0.3g, Fiber: 1.2g.

Tomatoes with Cauliflower Florets

Prep time + Cook time: 22 minutes , Servings: 4

5-Ingredients:

- ½ cup (chopped) scallions
- 1 pound cauliflower florets
- ½ cup chicken stock
- 2 cups (halved) cherry tomatoes
- 1 tbsp (chopped) chives
- 2 tbsp (chopped) parsley

What you'll need from the store cupboard:

- 1 tbsp avocado oil

Directions:

1. Let your Instant Pot preheat on Sauté mode.
2. Add oil and scallions, to sauté for 2 minutes.
3. Stir in remaining ingredients and mix well
4. Seal the pot's lid and cook for 10 minutes on manual mode at High.
5. Allow the pressure to release in 10 minutes naturally then remove the lid.
6. Serve fresh and enjoy.

Nutrition:

Calories 55, Total Fat: 1.6g, Carbs: 1.5g, Protein: 3.5g, Fiber: 0.4g.

Citrus Glazed Artichokes

Prep time + Cook time: 22 minutes , Servings: 4

5-Ingredients:

- 4 (trimmed) Artichokes
- 1 tbsp (chopped) Chives
- 1 tbsp (chopped) Parsley
- 1 tbsp Lemon juice

What you'll need from the store cupboard:

- 1 tbsp Olive oil
- 1 tbsp Sweet paprika
- 2 cups Water

Directions:

1. Toss the artichokes with all ingredients in a large bowl.
2. Pour water into the Instant Pot and place the steamer basket over it.
3. Place the artichokes in the steamer.
4. Seal the pot's lid and cook for 12 minutes on manual mode at High.
5. Allow the pressure to release in 10 minutes naturally then remove the lid.
6. Serve fresh and enjoy.

Nutrition:

Calories 113, Total Fat: 4g, Carbs: 3.5g, Protein: 5.6g, Fiber: 2.4g.

Paprika Zucchini

Prep time + Cook time: 30 minutes , Servings: 4

5-Ingredients:

- ½ cup Veggie stock
- 3 (sliced) Zucchinis
- 1 tbsp (chopped) Dill
- ½ tsp (grated) Nutmeg

What you'll need from the store cupboard:

- 2 tbsp Sweet paprika
- a pinch Salt and black pepper

Directions:

1. Add zucchinis along with remaining ingredients to the Instant Pot.
2. Seal the pot's lid and cook for 20 minutes on manual mode at Low.
3. Allow the pressure to release in 10 minutes naturally then remove the lid.
4. Serve fresh and enjoy.

Nutrition:

Calories 40, Total Fat: 2.3g, Carbs: 1.9g, Protein: 2.5g, Fiber: 1.5g.

Dill Mixed Fennel Bulbs

Prep time + Cook time: 20 minutes , Servings: 4

5-Ingredients:

- 2 (sliced) Fennel bulbs
- ¼ cup Chicken stock
- 1 tbsp (chopped) Dill
- 1 tbsp (chopped) Parsley

What you'll need from the store cupboard:

- a pinch Salt and black pepper

Directions:

1. Add fennel along with remaining ingredients to the Instant Pot.
2. Seal the pot's lid and cook for 10 minutes on manual mode at High.
3. Allow the pressure to release in 10 minutes naturally then remove the lid.
4. Serve fresh and enjoy.

Nutrition:

Calories 39, Total Fat: 3.2g, Carbs: 2.9g, Protein: 1.7g, Fiber: 1g.

Nutty Green Beans with Avocado

Prep time + Cook time: 25 minutes , Servings: 6

5-Ingredients:

- 2 cups (halved) Green beans
- ½ cup Chicken stock
- ½ cup (chopped) Walnuts
- 1 (peeled, pitted and cubed) Avocado

What you'll need from the store cupboard:

- 2 tsp Balsamic vinegar
- ¼ tsp Sweet paprika
- a pinch Salt and black pepper

Directions:

1. Add green beans, stock and remaining ingredients to the Instant Pot.
2. Seal the pot's lid and cook for 15 minutes on manual mode at High.
3. Allow the pressure to release in 10 minutes naturally then remove the lid.
4. Serve fresh and enjoy.

Nutrition:

Calories 146, Total Fat: 12.8g, Carbs: 6.7g, Protein: 3.9g, Fiber: 2.5g.

Thyme Mixed Brussels Sprouts

Prep time + Cook time: 22 minutes , Servings: 4

5-Ingredients:

- 2 and ½ lbs. (halved) Brussels sprouts
- 2 (chopped) Shallots
- ½ cups Beef stock
- 1 tbsp (chopped) Thyme

What you'll need from the store cupboard:

- 2 tbsp Olive oil
- a pinch Salt and black pepper

Directions:

1. Let your Instant Pot preheat on Sauté mode.
2. Add oil and shallot, to sauté for 2 minutes.
3. Stir in remaining ingredients and mix well.
4. Seal the pot's lid and cook for 10 minutes on manual mode at High.
5. Allow the pressure to release in 10 minutes naturally then remove the lid.
6. Serve fresh and enjoy.

Nutrition:

Calories 64, Total Fat: 7.1g, Carbs: 0.5g, Protein: 0.4g, Fiber: 0.3g.

Mashed Broccoli

Prep time + Cook time: 22 minutes , Servings: 4

5-Ingredients:

- 1 (florets separated) Broccoli
- ½ cup chicken stock
- 1 tbsp (chopped) chives
- 1 tbsp ghee (melted)

What you'll need from the store cupboard:

- ½ tsp turmeric powder
- a pinch Salt and black pepper

Directions:

1. Add broccoli along with remaining ingredients except ghee and chives to the Instant Pot.
2. Seal the pot's lid and cook for 12 minutes on manual mode at High.
3. Allow the pressure to release in 10 minutes naturally then remove the lid.
4. Transfer the broccoli mixture to the blender along with ghee.
5. Blend well until smooth then transfer the mixture to the serving plates.
6. Garnish with chives on top.
7. Serve fresh and enjoy.

Nutrition:
Calories 31, Total Fat: 3.3g, Carbs: 0.3g, Protein: 0.1g, Fiber: 0.1g.

Spiced Greens

Prep time + Cook time: 15 minutes , Servings: 4

5-Ingredients:

- 1 and ½ lbs. Baby spinach
- ½ pound (torn) Kale
- 1 cup Veggie stock
- 1 tbsp (chopped) Chives
- 1 tsp (ground) Nutmeg

What you'll need from the store cupboard:

- a pinch Salt and black pepper
- 1 tbsp (melted) Ghee

Directions:

1. Add spinach, kale and all the ingredients to the Instant Pot.
2. Seal the pot's lid and cook for 10 minutes on manual mode at High.
3. Allow the pressure to release in 10 minutes naturally then remove the lid.
4. Serve fresh and enjoy.

Nutrition:
Calories 59, Total Fat: 3.4g, Carbs: 2.4g, Protein: 1.8g, Fiber: 1g.

Tangy Thyme Tomatoes

Prep time + Cook time: 20 minutes , Servings: 4

5-Ingredients:

- ½ cup Veggie stock
- 1 pound (halved) Cherry tomatoes
- 1 Shallot (chopped)
- 1 tbsp (chopped) Thyme

What you'll need from the store cupboard:

- 1 tbsp Olive oil
- 1 tsp Chili powder
- a pinch Salt and black pepper

Directions:

1. Let your Instant Pot preheat on Sauté mode.
2. Add oil and shallot, to sauté for 2 minutes.
3. Stir in remaining ingredients and mix well.

4. Seal the pot's lid and cook for 8 minutes on manual mode at High.
5. Allow the pressure to release in 10 minutes naturally then remove the lid.
6. Serve fresh and enjoy.

Nutrition:
Calories 54, Total Fat: 3.9g, Carbs: 2.4g, Protein: 1.1g, Fiber: 1.8g.

Tomatoes and Olives Mix

Prep time + Cook time: 25 minutes , Servings: 4

5-Ingredients:
- 1 pound (halved) Cherry tomatoes
- 1 cup (pitted and halved) Kalamata olives
- 2 tbsp (crumbled) Goat cheese
- ¼ cup Veggie stock
- 1 tbsp (chopped) Chives

What you'll need from the store cupboard:
- 1 tbsp Balsamic vinegar
- a pinch Salt and black pepper

Directions:
1. Add olives, tomatoes and all the remaining ingredients except cheese and chives to the Instant Pot.
2. Seal the pot's lid and cook for 15 minutes on manual mode at High.
3. Allow the pressure to release in 10 minutes naturally then remove the lid.
4. Garnish with chives and cheese.
5. Serve fresh and enjoy.

Nutrition:
Calories 60, Total Fat: 3.8g, Carbs: 3.5g, Protein: 1.3g, Fiber: 2.1g.

Chili Cauliflower Spread

Prep time + Cook time: 25 minutes , Servings: 4

5-Ingredients:
- 1 (chopped) Shallot
- 1 pound Cauliflower florets
- ¼ cup Chicken stock
- 2 (chopped) Red hot chilies
- 2 tbsp (minced) Ginger

What you'll need from the store cupboard:
- 1 tbsp Avocado oil
- 1 and ¼ tbsp Balsamic vinegar

Directions:
1. Let your Instant Pot preheat on Sauté mode.
2. Add oil, ginger, and scallions, then sauté for 2 minutes.
3. Stir in remaining ingredients and mix well.
4. Seal the pot's lid and cook for 13 minutes on manual mode at High.
5. Allow the pressure to release in 10 minutes naturally then remove the lid.
6. Blend the mixture with a hand held blender until smooth.
7. Serve fresh and enjoy.

Nutrition:
Calories 45, Total Fat: 2.5g, Carbs: 2g, Protein: 2.6g, Fiber: 1.3g.

Balsamic Eggplant

Prep time + Cook time: 22 minutes , Servings: 4

5-Ingredients:
- 2 (sliced) Eggplants
- ¼ cup Veggie stock
- 1 tbsp (chopped) Chives
- 6 (minced) Garlic cloves

What you'll need from the store cupboard:
- 1 tbsp Balsamic vinegar
- 1 tbsp Olive oil
- a pinch Salt and black pepper

Directions:
1. Let your Instant Pot preheat on Sauté mode.
2. Add oil, and garlic, then sauté for 2 minutes.
3. Stir in remaining ingredients and mix well.
4. Seal the pot's lid and cook for 10 minutes on manual mode at High.
5. Allow the pressure to release in 10 minutes naturally then remove the lid.
6. Serve fresh and enjoy.

Nutrition:
Calories 106, Total Fat: 4g, Carbs: 2.7g, Protein: 3g, Fiber: 1.9g.

Artichokes Spread

Prep time + Cook time: 25 minutes , Servings: 6

5-Ingredients:
- 14 oz. (drained) Canned artichoke hearts
- 8 oz. (shredded) Mozzarella cheese
- 1 pound (torn)Spinach
- ½ cup Chicken stock
- ½ cup Coconut cream

What you'll need from the store cupboard:
- 1 tsp Garlic powder
- a pinch Salt and black pepper

Directions:
1. Add all the ingredients for the spread to the Instant Pot.
2. Seal the pot's lid and cook for 15 minutes on manual mode at High.
3. Allow the pressure to release in 10 minutes naturally then remove the lid.
4. Blend the mixture with a hand held blender until smooth.
5. Serve fresh and enjoy.

Nutrition:
Calories 204, Total Fat: 11.5g, Carbs: 4.2g, Protein: 5.9g, Fiber: 3.1g.

Butter Glazed Eggplants

Prep time + Cook time: 27 minutes , Servings: 4

5-Ingredients:
- 1 pound (sliced) Eggplants
- 2 (chopped) Shallots
- 1 cup Chicken stock
- 2 tbsp (chopped) Parsley

What you'll need from the store cupboard:
- a pinch Salt and black pepper
- 1 tbsp (melted) Ghee

Directions:
1. Let your Instant Pot preheat on Sauté mode.
2. Add ghee, and shallots, then sauté for 2 minutes.
3. Stir in eggplant and remaining ingredients and mix well.

4. Seal the pot's lid and cook for 10 minutes on manual mode at High.
5. Allow the pressure to release in 5 minutes naturally then remove the lid.
6. Serve fresh and enjoy.

Nutrition:
Calories 60, Total Fat: 3.5g, Carbs: 3g, Protein: 1.4g, Fiber: 1.8g.

Milky Bacon Artichokes

Prep time + Cook time: 22 minutes , Servings: 4

5-Ingredients:
- 1 cup (chopped) Bacon
- 1 pound (drained) Canned artichokes hearts
- ¼ tsp (ground) Nutmeg
- 1 cup Coconut milk
- 2 tbsp (chopped) Parsley

What you'll need from the store cupboard:
- a pinch Salt and black pepper

Directions:

1. Add artichokes and remaining ingredients to the Instant Pot.
2. Seal the pot's lid and cook for 12 minutes on manual mode at High.
3. Allow the pressure to release in 10 minutes naturally then remove the lid.
4. Serve fresh and enjoy.

Nutrition:
Calories 140, Total Fat: 14.2g, Carbs: 3.5g, Protein: 1.4g, Fiber: 1.4g.

Balsamic Glazed Greens

Prep time + Cook time: 25 minutes , Servings: 4

5-Ingredients:
- 1 bunch (trimmed) Collard greens
- ½ cup Chicken stock
- 1 tbsp (chopped) Chives
- 3 (minced) Garlic cloves

What you'll need from the store cupboard:
- 2 tbsp Avocado oil
- 2 tbsp Balsamic vinegar
- a pinch Salt and black pepper

Directions:
1. Let your Instant Pot preheat on Sauté mode.
2. Add oil, and garlic, then sauté for 2 minutes.
3. Stir in remaining ingredients and mix well.
4. Seal the pot's lid and cook for 13 minutes on manual mode at High.
5. Allow the pressure to release in 10 minutes naturally then remove the lid.
6. Serve fresh and enjoy.

Nutrition:
Calories 73, Total Fat: 2.1g, Carbs: 1.4g, Protein: 0.3g, Fiber: 0.3g.

Refreshing Cauliflower Rice

Prep time + Cook time: 25 minutes , Servings: 4

5-Ingredients:
- 1 (chopped) Shallot
- 1 and ½ cups Cauliflower rice
- 1 and ½ cups Chicken stock
- 2 tbsp (chopped) Chives
- 1 tsp (minced) Garlic

What you'll need from the store cupboard:
- 1 tbsp Avocado oil
- a pinch Salt and black pepper

Directions:
1. Let your Instant Pot preheat on Sauté mode.
2. Add oil, garlic, and shallot, then sauté for 2 minutes.
3. Stir in remaining ingredients and mix well.

4. Seal the pot's lid and cook for 13 minutes on manual mode at High.
5. Allow the pressure to release in 10 minutes naturally then remove the lid.
6. Serve fresh and enjoy.

Nutrition:
Calories 55, Total Fat: 2.3g, Carbs: 0.3g, Protein: 0.1g, Fiber: 0.2g.

Chili Leeks Satay

Prep time + Cook time: 20 minutes , Servings: 4

5-Ingredients:
- 2 (chopped) Scallions
- 4 (sliced) Leeks
- ¼ cup Chicken stock
- 2 tbsp (chopped) Parsley
- 1 tbsp (grated) Lemon zest

What you'll need from the store cupboard:
- 1 tsp Chili powder
- a pinch Salt and black pepper

Directions:

1. Add leeks and remaining ingredients to the Instant Pot.
2. Seal the pot's lid and cook for 10 minutes on manual mode at High.
3. Allow the pressure to release in 10 minutes naturally then remove the lid.
4. Serve fresh and enjoy.

Nutrition:
Calories 61, Total Fat: 2.5g, Carbs: 2.1g, Protein: 1.7g, Fiber: 1.1g.

Chili Mixed Cauliflower Rice

Prep time + Cook time: 30 minutes , Servings: 4

5-Ingredients:
- 2 tbsp (chopped) Green onions
- 1 cup Chicken stock
- 2 cups Cauliflower rice
- ½ tsp Cayenne pepper

What you'll need from the store cupboard:
- 1 tsp Chili powder
- a pinch Salt and black pepper

Directions:

1. Add cauliflower rice, stock and remaining ingredients to the Instant Pot.
2. Seal the pot's lid and cook for 20 minutes on manual mode at Low.
3. Allow the pressure to release in 10 minutes naturally then remove the lid.
4. Serve fresh and enjoy.

Nutrition:
Calories 52, Total Fat: 1.5g, Carbs: 0.3g, Protein: 0.7g, Fiber: 0.2g.

Cranberries Cauliflower

Prep time + Cook time: 25 minutes , Servings: 4

5-Ingredients:
- 2 (chopped) Shallots
- ½ cup Cranberries
- ½ cups Cauliflower rice

- 1 cup Veggie stock
- ½ cup (chopped) Cilantro

What you'll need from the store cupboard:

- 2 tbsp Avocado oil
- a pinch Salt and black pepper

Directions:
1. Let your Instant Pot preheat on Sauté mode.
2. Add oil, and shallot, then sauté for 2 minutes.
3. Stir in remaining ingredients and mix well.

4. Seal the pot's lid and cook for 13 minutes on manual mode at High.
5. Allow the pressure to release in 10 minutes naturally then remove the lid.
6. Serve fresh and enjoy.

Nutrition:
Calories 34, Total Fat: 2g, Carbs: 1.7g, Protein: 1g, Fiber: 0.2g.

Minty Balsamic Zucchinis

Prep time + Cook time: 22 minutes , Servings: 4

5-Ingredients:
- 2 (sliced) Zucchinis
- ¼ cup Chicken stock
- ½ cup (chopped) Green onions
- 2 tbsp (chopped) Mint
- 1 tsp Lime juice

What you'll need from the store cupboard:
- 1 tbsp Balsamic vinegar
- 1 tbsp Olive oil
- a pinch Salt and black pepper

Directions:
1. Let your Instant Pot preheat on Sauté mode.

2. Add oil, and onions, then sauté for 2 minutes.
3. Stir in remaining ingredients and mix well.
4. Seal the pot's lid and cook for 10 minutes on manual mode at High.
5. Allow the pressure to release in 10 minutes naturally then remove the lid.
6. Serve fresh and enjoy.

Nutrition:
Calories 52, Total Fat: 3.8g, Carbs: 2.3g, Protein: 1.6g, Fiber: 1.6g.

Spaghetti Squash

Prep Time + Cook time:10 minutes , Servings: 6

Ingredients:
- 1 (4-pound) spaghetti squash
- 1 cup water

What you'll need from the store cupboard:
- Salt and pepper
- 1 to 2 tablespoons butter

Directions:
1. Cut the spaghetti squash in half and remove the seeds.
2. Place the squash in the Instant Pot and add the water.
3. Close and lock the lid, then press the Manual button and adjust the timer to 5 minutes.

4. When the timer goes off, do a Quick Release by pressing Cancel and switching the steam valve to "venting."
5. When the pot has depressurized, open the lid.
6. Remove the squash and scrape the flesh into a bowl with two forks.
7. Stir in the butter and season with salt and pepper to serve.

Nutrition:
calories 70 fat 4g ,protein 1g ,carbs 8g ,fiber 1.5g ,net carbs 6.5g

Lemon Parmesan Zucchini "Noodles"

Prep Time + Cook time:8 minutes , Servings: 4

Ingredients:

- 3 large zucchini, spiralized into noodles
- ½ cup grated parmesan cheese

What you'll need from the store cupboard:

- 1 tablespoon olive oil
- 3 cloves minced garlic
- 2 tablespoons fresh lemon juice
- 1 tablespoon fresh lemon zest

Directions:

1. Turn the Instant Pot on to the Sauté setting and let it heat up.
2. Add the olive oil then stir in the garlic and lemon zest.
3. Cook for 60 seconds, then stir in the zucchini noodles and lemon juice.
4. Cook for 2 minutes until the noodles are just tender.
5. Stir in the parmesan cheese and serve hot.

Nutrition:

calories 125 fat 7g ,protein 7g ,carbs 9.5g ,fiber 3g ,net carbs 6.5g

Garlic Asparagus

Prep Time + Cook time:7 minutes , Servings: 4

Ingredients:

- 1 pound asparagus
- 1 cup water

What you'll need from the store cupboard:

- 2 cloves minced garlic
- 1 tablespoon butter
- Salt and pepper

Directions:

1. Place a steamer insert in the Instant Pot and add the water.
2. Add the asparagus to the steamer insert, then close and lock the lid.
3. Press the Steam button and set the timer to 2 minutes.
4. When the timer goes off, do a Quick Release by pressing Cancel and switching the steam valve to "venting".
5. When the pot has depressurized, open the lid.
6. Remove the steamer insert and set the asparagus aside.
7. Press the Sauté button and add the butter and garlic.
8. Cook for 1 to 2 minutes then toss in the asparagus.
9. Season with salt and pepper to serve.

Nutrition:

calories 50 fat 3g ,protein 2.5g ,carbs 5g ,fiber 2.5g ,net carbs 2.5g

Creamy Mashed Cauliflower

Prep Time + Cook time:8 minutes , Servings: 4

Ingredients:

- 1 cup water
- 2 medium heads cauliflower, chopped

What you'll need from the store cupboard:

- Salt and pepper
- 2 tablespoons butter

Directions:

1. Place the steamer insert in the Instant Pot and add the water.
2. Add the cauliflower to the steamer insert.
3. Close and lock the lid, then press Manual and cook on high pressure for 3 minutes.
4. When the timer goes off, do a Quick Release by pressing Cancel and switching the steam valve to "venting."
5. When the pot has depressurized, open the lid.
6. Transfer the cauliflower to a food processor and add the butter, salt, and pepper.
7. Blend until the cauliflower is smooth then spoon into a bowl to serve.

Nutrition:

calories 125 fat 6g ,protein 6g ,carbs 15g ,fiber 7g ,net carbs 8g

Garlic Green Beans

Prep Time + Cook time:10 minutes , Servings: 4

Ingredients:

- 1 pound green beans, sliced
- 1 cup water

What you'll need from the store cupboard:

- Salt and pepper
- 3 cloves minced garlic
- 2 tablespoons butter

Directions:

1. Place the green beans in the Instant Pot.
2. Add the water, butter, and garlic then stir well.
3. Close and lock the lid, then press the Manual button and cook on Low Pressure for 5 minutes.
4. When the timer goes off, do a Quick Release by pressing Cancel and switching the steam valve to "venting."
5. When the pot has depressurized, open the lid.
6. Season the beans with salt and pepper and serve hot.

Nutrition:

calories 90 fat 6g ,protein 2g ,carbs 8.5g ,fiber 4g ,net carbs 4.5g

Chapter 9 Salad & Salsa Recipes

Cod Beans Salad

Prep time + Cook time: 25 minutes , Servings: 4

5-Ingredients:

- 1 pound (skinless, boneless and cubed) Cod fillets
- 2 tbsp (chopped) Parsley
- 2 cups (trimmed and halved) Green beans
- 1 tbsp (chopped) Chives
- 1 cup Coconut cream

What you'll need from the store cupboard:

- a pinch Salt and black pepper
- 2 tsp Lime juice
- 1 tbsp (chopped) Oregano

Directions:

1. Add green beans and other ingredients except for the chives and oregano.
2. Seal the pot's lid and cook for 15 minutes on manual mode at High.
3. Allow the pressure to release in 10 minutes naturally then remove the lid.
4. Garnish with chives and oregano.
5. Serve fresh and enjoy.

Nutrition:

Calories 160, Total Fat: 14.5g, Carbs: 8.1g, Protein: 2.6g, Fiber: 3.8g.

Mushroom Cheese Salad

Prep time + Cook time: 20 minutes , Servings: 4

5-Ingredients:

- 4 (cubed) Tomatoes
- ½ cup Veggie stock
- 1 pound (halved) Mushrooms
- 1 cup (shredded) Mozzarella
- 1 tbsp (chopped)Parsley

What you'll need from the store cupboard:

- a pinch Salt and black pepper
- 1 tbsp (melted) Ghee

Directions:

1. Let your Instant Pot preheat on Sauté mode.
2. Add ghee and mushrooms, then sauté for 2 minutes.
3. Stir in remaining ingredients except for mozzarella and mix well.
4. Drizzle mozzarella cheese over this mixture.
5. Seal the pot's lid and cook for 8 minutes on manual mode at High.
6. Allow the pressure to release in 10 minutes naturally then remove the lid.
7. Serve fresh and enjoy.

Nutrition:

Calories 95, Total Fat: 5g, Carbs: 4.7g, Protein: 6.7g, Fiber: 2.3g.

Mussels Spinach Salad

Prep time + Cook time: 16 minutes , Servings: 4

5-Ingredients:

- 1 pound (scrubbed) Mussels
- 2 cups Baby spinach
- ½ cup Chicken stock
- 2 (chopped) Scallions
- ½ tsp (chopped) Oregano

What you'll need from the store cupboard:

- 1 tbsp Balsamic vinegar
- a pinch Salt and black pepper

- ½ tsp Olive oil
- ½ tsp Chili powder

Directions:
1. Add mussels, stock, salt, and black pepper to the Instant Pot.
2. Seal the pot's lid and cook for 6 minutes on manual mode at High.
3. Allow the pressure to release in 10 minutes naturally then remove the lid.
4. Toss the mussels with other ingredients in a bowl.
5. Serve fresh and enjoy.

Nutrition:
Calories 112, Total Fat: 3.4g, Carbs: 1.7g, Protein: 14.1g, Fiber: 0.7g.

Salmon Radish Salad

Prep time + Cook time: 25 minutes , Servings: 4

5-Ingredients:
- 1 pound (boneless, skinless and cubed) Salmon fillets
- 2 cups (sliced) Red radishes
- 1 (sliced) Shallot
- ½ cup Coconut cream
- 2 tbsp (chopped) Mint leaves

What you'll need from the store cupboard:
- ½ tbsp Avocado oil
- a pinch Salt and black pepper

Directions:
1. Let your Instant Pot preheat on Sauté mode.
2. Add oil, and shallot, then sauté for 2 minutes.
3. Place the salmon and cook for another 2 minutes.
4. Stir in remaining ingredients and mix well.
5. Seal the pot's lid and cook for 10 minutes on manual mode at High.
6. Allow the pressure to release in 10 minutes naturally then remove the lid.
7. Serve fresh and enjoy.

Nutrition:
Calories 232, Total Fat: 14.5g, Carbs: 4g, Protein: 23.2g, Fiber: 1.9g.

Salmon Chard Salad

Prep time + Cook time: 25 minutes , Servings: 4

5-Ingredients:
- 1 pound (boneless, skinless and cubed) Salmon fillets
- ¼ pound (torn) Swiss chard
- 1 (chopped) Spring onion
- ¼ cup Chicken stock

What you'll need from the store cupboard:
- a pinch Salt and black pepper
- 1 tsp Olive oil
- 1 tbsp Lime juice
- 1 tbsp (chopped) Rosemary

Directions:
1. Let your Instant Pot preheat on Sauté mode.
2. Add oil, and spring onion, then sauté for 2 minutes.
3. Place salmon in the pot and cook for 2 minutes per side.
4. Stir in remaining ingredients and mix well.
5. Seal the pot's lid and cook for 10 minutes on manual mode at High.
6. Allow the pressure to release in 10 minutes naturally then remove the lid.
7. Serve fresh and enjoy.

Nutrition:
Calories 170, Total Fat: 8.4g, Carbs: 1.9g, Protein: 22.7g, Fiber: 0.9g.

Chicken Pesto Salad

Prep time + Cook time: 30 minutes , Servings: 4

5-Ingredients:
- 1 pound (skinless, boneless and cubed) Chicken breast
- 2 (chopped) Spring onions
- 1 cup Chicken stock
- 1 cup (crushed) Tomatoes
- 2 Garlic cloves, chopped

What you'll need from the store cupboard:
- 2 tbsp Olive oil
- 1 tbsp Oregano, chopped
- 2 tbsp Basil pesto

Directions:
1. Let your Instant Pot preheat on Sauté mode.
2. Add oil, chicken, and onions, then sauté for 5 minutes.
3. Stir in remaining ingredients except for basil and mix well.
4. Seal the pot's lid and cook for 15 minutes on manual mode at High.
5. Allow the pressure to release in 10 minutes naturally then remove the lid.
6. Serve fresh and enjoy.

Nutrition:
Calories 212, Total Fat: 10.2g, Carbs: 4.6g, Protein: 25.2g, Fiber: 1.3g.

Spinach Cabbage Salad

Prep time + Cook time: 25 minutes , Servings: 4

5-Ingredients:
- 2 cups (shredded) Red cabbage
- 1 (chopped) Spring onion
- 1 pound Baby spinach
- ½ cup Chicken stock
- 1 tbsp (chopped) Chives

What you'll need from the store cupboard:
- 1 tbsp Avocado oil
- 1 tsp Chili powder
- 1 tbsp Sweet paprika
- 1 tbsp Avocado mayonnaise

Directions:
1. Let your Instant Pot preheat on Sauté mode.
2. Add oil, and onion, then sauté for 2 minutes.
3. Stir in remaining ingredients except for spinach, chives, and mayo and mix well.
4. Seal the pot's lid and cook for 12 minutes on manual mode at High.
5. Allow the pressure to release in 10 minutes naturally then remove the lid.
6. Add spinach, chives, and mayonnaise then mix well.
7. Serve fresh and enjoy.

Nutrition:
Calories 72, Total Fat: 3.8g, Carbs: 2.6g, Protein: 4.3g, Fiber: 1.2g.

Shrimp Mussels Salad

Prep time + Cook time: 18 minutes , Servings: 4

5-Ingredients:
- 1 pound (scrubbed) Mussels
- ¼ cup Chicken stock
- 1 pound (peeled and deveined) Shrimp
- 1 and ½ cups Baby spinach
- 1 tbsp (chopped) Parsley

What you'll need from the store cupboard:
- 2 tbsp Olive oil
- 1 tsp Hot paprika
- 2 tsp (dried) Oregano
- ½ cup Tomato passata

Directions:

1. Add mussels and all other ingredients except parsley and spinach to the Instant Pot.
2. Seal the pot's lid and cook for 10 minutes on manual mode at High.
3. Allow the pressure to release in 6 minutes quickly then remove the lid.
4. Add parsley and spinach to the cooked mixture.
5. Stir cook for 2 minutes on Sauté mode.
6. Serve fresh and enjoy.

Nutrition:
Calories 303, Total Fat: 11.7g, Carbs: 7.8g, Protein: 39.3g, Fiber: 0.8g.

Radish Shrimp Salad

Prep time + Cook time: 20 minutes , Servings: 4

5-Ingredients:
- 1 pound (peeled and deveined) Shrimp
- 1 (chopped) Shallot
- 2 cups (sliced) Radishes
- 1 cup (cooked and crumbled) Bacon
- 1 cup Veggie stock

What you'll need from the store cupboard:
- a pinch Salt and black pepper
- 1 tbsp Olive oil
- 1 tsp Sweet paprika
- 1 tbsp (chopped) Oregano

Directions:

1. Let your Instant Pot preheat on Sauté mode.
2. Add oil, and shallots, then sauté for 2 minutes.
3. Stir in remaining ingredients except for bacon and oregano and mix well.
4. Seal the pot's lid and cook for 13 minutes on manual mode at High.
5. Allow the pressure to release in 5 minutes quickly then remove the lid.
6. Top the mixture with oregano and bacon.
7. Serve fresh and enjoy.

Nutrition:
Calories 179, Total Fat: 5.7g, Carbs: 4.5g, Protein: 26.5g, Fiber: 1.6g.

Basic Mushrooms Salsa

Prep time + Cook time: 20 minutes , Servings: 4

5-Ingredients:
- 1 pound (halved) White mushrooms
- ¼ cup Chicken stock
- 2 (cubed) Tomatoes
- 1 (peeled, pitted and cubed) Avocado

What you'll need from the store cupboard:
- a pinch Salt and black pepper
- 1 tbsp (melted) Ghee
- 1 tbsp (chopped) Oregano
- 1 tbsp (chopped) Basil
- 1 tbsp (chopped) Rosemary

Directions:
1. Add mushrooms and all other ingredients to the Instant Pot.
2. Seal the pot's lid and cook for 10 minutes on manual mode at High.
3. Allow the pressure to release in 10 minutes naturally then remove the lid.
4. Serve fresh and enjoy.

Nutrition:
Calories 173, Total Fat: 13.7g, Carbs: 7.7g, Protein: 5.3g, Fiber: 6.2g.

Peppers Avocado Salsa

Prep time + Cook time: 22 minutes , Servings: 4

5-Ingredients:
- 1 and ½ lbs. (cut into strips) Mixed bell peppers
- 2 tbsp (chopped) Parsley
- 2 (cubed) Tomatoes
- 1 (peeled, pitted and cubed) Avocado

What you'll need from the store cupboard:
- 1 tbsp Avocado oil
- a pinch Salt and black pepper
- 2 tsp Lime juice
- 2 tbsp (chopped) Basil
- ½ cup Tomato passata

Directions:
1. Add bell peppers and all other ingredients to the Instant Pot.
2. Seal the pot's lid and cook for 12 minutes on manual mode at High.
3. Allow the pressure to release in 10 minutes naturally then remove the lid.
4. Serve fresh and enjoy.

Nutrition:
Calories 127, Total Fat: 10.5g, Carbs: 7.8g, Protein: 2g, Fiber: 4.8g.

Zucchini Tomato Salsa

Prep time + Cook time: 20 minutes , Servings: 4

5-Ingredients:
- 1 pound (cubed) Tomatoes
- 2 (cubed) Zucchinis
- ¼ cup Chicken stock
- 1 tbsp (chopped) Cilantro

What you'll need from the store cupboard:
- 2 tbsp Olive oil
- ½ tsp Red pepper flakes
- 2 tsp (chopped) Ginger
- 2 tsp (minced) Garlic
- 2 tsp (dried) Oregano

Directions:
1. Let your Instant Pot preheat on Sauté mode.
2. Add oil, pepper flakes, ginger, and garlic, then sauté for 2 minutes.
3. Stir in remaining ingredients and mix well.
4. Seal the pot's lid and cook for 8 minutes on manual mode at High.
5. Allow the pressure to release in 10 minutes naturally then remove the lid.
6. Serve fresh and enjoy.

Nutrition:
Calories 105, Total Fat: 7.6g, Carbs: 6.7g, Protein: 2.5g, Fiber: 3g.

Walnuts Zucchinis Salsa

Prep time + Cook time: 22 minutes , Servings: 4

5-Ingredients:
- 4 (sliced) Zucchinis
- ½ cup Veggie stock
- 1 cup (chopped) Walnuts
- ¼ cup (chopped) Parsley
- ¼ cup (grated) Parmesan cheese

What you'll need from the store cupboard:
- 1 tsp Balsamic vinegar
- 1 tbsp (melted) Ghee
- 3 (minced) Garlic cloves
- 1 tsp (dried) Oregano

Directions:
1. Add zucchinis and other ingredients except for parmesan to the Instant Pot.
2. Seal the pot's lid and cook for 12 minutes on manual mode at High.
3. Allow the pressure to release in 10 minutes naturally then remove the lid.
4. Garnish with parmesan cheese.
5. Serve fresh and enjoy.

Nutrition:
Calories 259, Total Fat: 22.1g, Carbs: 5.9g, Protein: 10.2g, Fiber: 4.6g.

Chapter 10 Dip & Dressing Recipes

Zucchini Dip

Prep time + Cook time: 20 minutes , Servings: 4

5-Ingredients:

- 1 (chopped) Shallot
- 1 and ½ lbs. (chopped) Zucchinis
- ¼ cup Veggie stock
- 2 (minced) Garlic cloves

What you'll need from the store cupboard:

- a pinch Salt and black pepper
- 1 tbsp Olive oil
- 1 bunch (chopped) Basil

Directions:

1. Let your Instant Pot preheat on Sauté mode.
2. Add oil, garlic, and shallot, then sauté for 2 minutes.
3. Stir in remaining ingredients and mix well.
4. Seal the pot's lid and cook for 8 minutes on manual mode at High.
5. Allow the pressure to release in 10 minutes naturally then remove the lid.
6. Blend the mixture in a food processor until smooth.
7. Serve fresh and enjoy.

Nutrition:

Calories 75, Total Fat: 2.5g, Carbs: 0.6g, Protein: 1.2g, Fiber: 0.1g.

Spinach Leeks Dip

Prep time + Cook time: 30 minutes , Servings: 4

5-Ingredients:

- 1 (chopped) Shallot
- 2 (chopped) Leeks
- 4 cups (torn) Spinach
- ¼ cup Veggie stock
- 2 (minced) Garlic cloves

What you'll need from the store cupboard:

- 2 tbsp Avocado oil
- a pinch Salt and black pepper
- ¼ cup Lime juice
- 1 bunch (chopped) Basil

Directions:

1. Let your Instant Pot preheat on Sauté mode.
2. Add oil, garlic, leeks, and shallot, then sauté for 5 minutes.
3. Stir in remaining ingredients and mix well.
4. Seal the pot's lid and cook for 15 minutes on manual mode at High.
5. Allow the pressure to release in 10 minutes naturally then remove the lid.
6. Blend the cooked mixture using a handheld blender until smooth.
7. Serve fresh and enjoy.

Nutrition:

Calories 56, Total Fat: 1.8g, Carbs: 1.6g, Protein: 1.7g, Fiber: 0.5g.

Tomato Zucchini Dip

Prep time + Cook time: 25 minutes , Servings: 4

5-Ingredients:

- 2 cups (cubed) Tomatoes
- 2 cups (cubed) Zucchinis
- 2 (chopped) Red chilies
- ¼ cup Veggie stock
- 2 (chopped) Scallions

What you'll need from the store cupboard:

- a pinch Salt and black pepper
- 1 tbsp Olive oil
- 1 tbsp Hot paprika
- 1 tbsp (chopped) Basil

Directions:

1. Let your Instant Pot preheat on Sauté mode.
2. Add oil, chilies, and scallions, then sauté for 2 minutes.
3. Stir in remaining ingredients and mix well.
4. Seal the pot's lid and cook for 12 minutes on manual mode at High.
5. Allow the pressure to release in 10 minutes naturally then remove the lid.
6. Blend the mixture with a hand held blender until smooth.
7. Garnish with basil leaves.
8. Serve fresh and enjoy.

Nutrition:

Calories 58, Total Fat: 3.5g, Carbs: 2.3g, Protein: 1.6g, Fiber: 1.9g.

Eggplant Green Dip

Prep time + Cook time: 25 minutes , Servings: 4

5-Ingredients:

- 2 cubed Eggplants
- 1 cup Baby spinach
- ¼ cup Veggie stock
- 1 tbsp Lemon juice
- ¼ cup Coconut cream

What you'll need from the store cupboard:

- A pinch Salt and black pepper
- 2 minced Garlic cloves

Directions:

1. Add eggplants, spinach and all other ingredients to the Instant Pot.
2. Seal the pot's lid and cook for 15 minutes on manual mode at High.
3. Allow the pressure to release in 10 minutes naturally then remove the lid.
4. Blend this mixture using a hand held blender until smooth.
5. Serve fresh and enjoy.

Nutrition:

Calories 108, Total Fat: 4.1g, Carbs: 3.7g, Protein: 3.5g, Fiber: 2.6g.

Basil and Mustard Greens Dip

Prep time + Cook time: 19 minutes , Servings: 4

5-Ingredients:

- ¼ cup Veggie stock
- 6 oz. (chopped) Mustard greens
- 2 tbsp Coconut cream
- 1 (minced) Garlic clove

What you'll need from the store cupboard:

- 1 tbsp Balsamic vinegar
- a pinch Salt and black pepper
- 1 tbsp Olive oil
- 1 tbsp (chopped) Basil

Directions:

1. Let your Instant Pot preheat on Sauté mode.
2. Add oil, and garlic, then sauté for 1 minute.
3. Stir in remaining ingredients and mix well.
4. Seal the pot's lid and cook for 13 minutes on manual mode at High.
5. Allow the pressure to release in 5 minutes naturally then remove the lid.
6. Blend the mixture with a hand held blender until smooth.
7. Serve fresh and enjoy.

Nutrition:
Calories 60, Total Fat: 5.4g, Carbs: 2.8g, Protein: 1.4g, Fiber: 1.6g.

Broccoli Yogurt Dip

Prep time + Cook time: 25 minutes , Servings: 6

5-Ingredients:

- 2 cups Veggie stock
- 6 cups Broccoli florets
- 1 cup Greek yogurt
- 1 tbsp (chopped) Dill
- ½ cup Coconut cream

What you'll need from the store cupboard:

- 2 tbsp Avocado oil
- a pinch Salt and black pepper
- 8 (minced) Garlic cloves

Directions:

1. Let your Instant Pot preheat on Sauté mode.
2. Add oil, and garlic, then sauté for 2 minutes.
3. Stir in remaining ingredients except for yogurt and dill and mix well
4. Seal the pot's lid and cook for 13 minutes on manual mode at High.
5. Allow the pressure to release in 10 minutes naturally then remove the lid.
6. Add yogurt and blend the mixture with a hand held blender until smooth.
7. Garnish with dill then serve fresh.

Nutrition:
Calories 136, Total Fat: 8.6g, Carbs: 5.6g, Protein: 5.1g, Fiber: 4.8g.

Basil Peppers Dip

Prep time + Cook time: 20 minutes , Servings: 2

5-Ingredients:
- ½ cup Lemon juice
- 3 (minced) Shallots
- 1 and ½ lbs. (roughly chopped) Mixed peppers
- ¼ cup Chicken stock

What you'll need from the store cupboard:
- 1 tbsp Balsamic vinegar
- 1 tbsp Olive oil
- ½ tsp Hot sauce
- 2 tbsp (chopped) Basil

Directions:
1. Let your Instant Pot preheat on Sauté mode.
2. Add oil, and shallots, then sauté for 2 minutes.
3. Stir in remaining ingredients and mix well.
4. Seal the pot's lid and cook for 13 minutes on manual mode at High.
5. Allow the pressure to release in 5 minutes quickly then remove the lid.
6. Use an immersion blender to blend the cooked mixture until smooth
7. Serve fresh and enjoy.

Nutrition:
Calories 78, Total Fat: 7.6g, Carbs: 1.5g, Protein: 0.7g, Fiber: 0.3g.

Olives Coconut Dip

Prep time + Cook time: 15 minutes , Servings: 4

5-Ingredients:
- 4 cups Baby spinach
- 1 tbsp (chopped) Chives
- 1 cup (pitted and halved) Kalamata olives
- ½ cup Coconut cream

What you'll need from the store cupboard:
- 2 tbsp Avocado oil
- a pinch Salt and black pepper
- 2 tbsp Lime juice
- 4 (roasted and minced) Garlic cloves

Directions:
1. Add avocado oil and all other ingredients except chives to the Instant Pot.
2. Seal the pot's lid and cook for 10 minutes on manual mode at High.
3. Allow the pressure to release in 5 minutes naturally then remove the lid.
4. Use an immersion blender to blend the cooked mixture until smooth.
5. Garnish with chives.
6. Serve fresh and enjoy.

Nutrition:
Calories 129, Total Fat: 11.8g, Carbs: 6.3g, Protein: 2.1g, Fiber: 2.8g.

Chapter 11 Keto Bowls Recipes

Spicy Shrimp And Eggplant Bowls

Prep Time + Cook time: 20 minutes , Servings: 4

5-Ingredients:
- 2 Cubed eggplants
- 1 lime; juiced
- 1 lb. Shrimp; peeled and deveined
- 2 tbsp Veggie stock
- 4 Minced garlic cloves

What you'll need from the store cupboard:
- A pinch of salt and black pepper
- 2 tbsp Olive oil
- ½ tsp Sweet paprika
- 2 tbsp Chopped basil

Directions:

1. Press 'Sauté' on the instant pot and add the oil. When hot, add the eggplants and the garlic to cook for 2 minutes.
2. Mix in the basil, paprika, lime juice, shrimp, veggie stock, salt, and pepper then seal the lid to cook for 8 minutes on low pressure.
3. Natural release the pressure for 10 minutes, then share it into bowls and serve.

Nutrition
Calories 269, fat 9.5, carbs 6.7, protein 28.8, fiber 5.4

Chili Shrimp With Olives Bowls

Prep Time + Cook time: 20 minutes , Servings: 4

5-Ingredients:
- ½ cup Chicken stock
- 1 ½ lbs. Shrimp; peeled and deveined
- 2 Cubed tomatoes
- 1 lb. Black olives; pitted and halved
- 2 Chopped scallions

What you'll need from the store cupboard:
- 2 tbsp Olive oil
- 1 tbsp Sweet paprika

Directions:

1. Press 'Sauté' on the instant pot and add the oil. When hot, cook the scallions for 2 minutes.
2. Mix in the remaining ingredients, then seal the lid to cook for 8 minutes on low pressure.
3. Natural release the pressure for 10 minutes, dish into bowls and serve.

Nutrition
Calories 118, fat 11, carbs 6.1, protein 1.3, fiber 2.7

Turkey With Celery And Tomatoes Bowls

Prep Time + Cook time: 30 minutes , Servings: 4

5-Ingredients:
- 1 Skinless, boneless and cubed turkey breast
- 1 tbsp Chopped cilantro .
- 2 cups Chopped tomatoes
- 2 cups Chicken stock
- 1 Chopped celery stalk

What you'll need from the store cupboard:
- A pinch of salt and black pepper

- 1 tbsp Avocado oil
- 1 tsp Olive oil

Directions:
1. Press 'Sauté' on the instant pot and add the oil. When it is hot, add the turkey meat to cook for 5 minutes.
2. Mix in the cilantro, tomatoes, stock, celery, salt, and pepper then seal the lid to cook for 15 minutes at high pressure.
3. Natural release the pressure for 10 minutes, ladle into bowls and serve.

Nutrition
Calories 81, fat 4.3, carbs 6, protein 8.6, fiber 1.5

Spicy Veggie Bowls

Prep Time + Cook time: 30 minutes , Servings: 4

5-Ingredients:
- 1 tbsp Chopped parsley
- 1 Chopped shallot
- 1 lb. Torn kale
- 20 oz Chopped canned tomatoes
- ½ tsp Cayenne pepper

What you'll need from the store cupboard:
- A pinch of salt and black pepper
- 2 tbsp Olive oil
- 2 cloves Minced garlic

Directions:
1. Press 'Sauté' on the instant pot and add the oil. When it is hot, add the garlic and shallot to cook for 2 minutes.
2. Mix in the kale, tomatoes, salt and pepper, cayenne pepper, and parsley, then seal the lid o cook for 18 minutes at high pressure.
3. Natural release the pressure for 10 minutes, ladle into bowls and serve.

Nutrition
Calories 145, fat 7.3, carbs 5.2, protein 4.8, fiber 3.5

Passata Mussels Bowls

Prep time + Cook time: 20 minutes , Servings: 4

5-Ingredients:
- 2 lbs. (scrubbed) Mussels
- 2 (chopped) Chili peppers
- ¼ cup Veggie stock

What you'll need from the store cupboard:
- ¼ cup Balsamic vinegar
- a pinch Salt and black pepper
- 1 tbsp Olive oil
- 2 (minced) Garlic cloves
- ½ cup (chopped) Oregano
- 2 cups Tomato passata

Directions:
1. Let your Instant Pot preheat on Sauté mode.
2. Add oil, garlic and chili peppers, then sauté for 2 minutes.
3. Stir in remaining ingredients and mix well.
4. Seal the pot's lid and cook for 8 minutes on manual mode at High.
5. Allow the pressure to release in 10 minutes naturally then remove the lid.
6. Serve fresh and enjoy.

Nutrition:
Calories 306, Total Fat: 9.8g, Carbs: 6.5g, Protein: 20.5g, Fiber: 4.8g.

Savory Shrimp Bowls

Prep time + Cook time: 10 minutes , Servings: 6

5-Ingredients:

- 2 lbs. (peeled and deveined) Shrimp
- 2 (chopped) Scallions
- 1 cup Veggie stock
- 1 (peeled, pitted and cubed) Avocado

What you'll need from the store cupboard:

- 1 tbsp Olive oil
- 1 tbsp Sweet paprika
- 2 (minced) Garlic cloves

Directions:

1. Let your Instant Pot preheat on Sauté mode.
2. Add oil, garlic and scallions, then sauté for 1 minute.
3. Stir in remaining ingredients and mix well.
4. Seal the pot's lid and cook for 4 minutes on manual mode at High.
5. Allow the pressure to release in 5 minutes naturally then remove the lid.
6. Serve fresh and enjoy.

Nutrition:
Calories 274, Total Fat: 11.6g, Carbs: 6.5g, Protein: 35.4g, Fiber: 2.8g.

Shrimp with Okra Bowls

Prep time + Cook time: 22 minutes , Servings: 4

5-Ingredients:

- 1 pound (trimmed) Okra
- ½ pound (peeled and deveined) Shrimp
- 1 tbsp (chopped) Cilantro

What you'll need from the store cupboard:

- a pinch Salt and black pepper
- 2 tbsp Olive oil
- 1 cup (chopped) Tomato passata

Directions:

1. Add shrimp, okra and all other ingredients to the Instant Pot.
2. Seal the pot's lid and cook for 12 minutes on manual mode at High.
3. Allow the pressure to release in 5 minutes naturally then remove the lid.
4. Serve fresh and enjoy.

Nutrition:
Calories 188, Total Fat: 8.3g, Carbs: 6.1g, Protein: 15.6g, Fiber: 4.6g.

Almonds and Chicken Bowl

Prep Time + Cook time: 40 minutes , Servings: 8

5-Ingredients:

- half cup Almonds
- 1 lb. Brussels sprouts
- 2 pieces Scallions
- 2 lbs. (no bones and skin) Chicken breasts

What you'll need from the store cupboard:

- Salt and Black pepper to taste
- 2 tbsp Olive oil
- 1 tsp Sweet paprika
- 1 tsp Thyme

Directions:

1. Put the instant pot on Sauté option, then put the oil and cook it. After that, put the meat and scallions then heat it for 5 minutes.
2. Put the other ingredients, then cover it and heat it for 25 minutes on high temperature.

3. Release the pressure gradually for 10 minutes, then after that split them among your plates before eating.

Nutritional Info per Servings:
Calories: 307, Fat: 15.1g, Fiber: 3.1g, Carbs: 6.6g, Protein: 36.1g

Duck and Shallots Bowl

Prep Time + Cook time: 35 minutes , Servings: 4
5-Ingredients:
- 1 cup Chicken stock
- 1 piece Shallot
- 2 pieces (no bones and skin) Duck legs
- 1 cup Heavy cream

What you'll need from the store cupboard:
- Salt and Black pepper to taste
- 1 tbsp Melted ghee
- 1 and 1/2 tsp Chili paste
- 2 tsp Thyme

Directions:

1. Put the instant pot on Sauté option, then put the ghee and cook it. After that, put the meat and shallot then heat it for 5 minutes.
2. Put the other ingredients, then cover it and heat it for 25 minutes on high temperature.
3. Release the pressure gradually for 10 minutes, then after that split them among your plates before eating.

Nutritional Info per Servings:
Calories: 337, Fat: 21.2g, Fiber: 0.2g, Carbs: 1.4g, Protein: 33.6g

Salmon Bowls

Prep time + Cook time: 13 minutes , Servings: 4
5-Ingredients:
- 1 cup (drained) Canned artichoke hearts
- 1 pound (skinless, boneless and cubed) Smoked salmon
- 1 cup (cubed) Cherry tomatoes
- 1 tbsp (chopped) Chives
- ¼ cup Coconut cream

What you'll need from the store cupboard:
- a pinch Salt and black pepper
- 1 tbsp Olive oil

Directions:

1. Add salmon, artichokes and remaining ingredients to the Instant Pot.
2. Seal the pot's lid and cook for 8 minutes on manual mode at High.
3. Allow the pressure to release in 5 minutes naturally then remove the lid.
4. Serve fresh and enjoy.

Nutrition:
Calories 206, Total Fat: 12.4g, Carbs: 2.6g, Protein: 21.5g, Fiber: 0.9g.

Chapter 12 Dessert Recipes

Maple Almond Cake in a Jar

Prep Time + Cook time:15 minutes , Servings: 3

Ingredients:

- 3 large eggs

What you'll need from the store cupboard:

- ¼ teaspoon salt
- 1 cup almond flour
- 1 ½ teaspoons vanilla extract
- 3 tablespoons sugar-free maple syrup
- 1 cup of water

Directions:

1. Place the trivet in the Instant Pot and add 1 cup of water.
2. Whisk together the almond flour, egg, sugar-free maple syrup, vanilla, and salt in a mixing bowl.
3. Divide the mixture among three 8-ounce jars.
4. Cover the jars with foil then place on the trivet, close and lock the lid.
5. Press the Manual button and adjust the timer to 10 minutes.
6. When the timer goes off, do a Quick Release by pressing Cancel and switching the steam valve to "venting."
7. When the pot has depressurized, open the lid.
8. Remove the jars and let them cool a little before serving.

Nutrition:

calories 275 fat 22.5g ,protein 13.5g ,carbs 7g ,fiber 3.5g ,net carbs 3.5g

Coconut Flan

Prep Time + Cook time:29 minutes , Servings: 6

Ingredients:

- 2 tablespoons water
- 1 cup unsweetened coconut milk
- 3 large eggs

What you'll need from the store cupboard:

- Pinch salt
- 1 cup heavy cream
- ¾ cup powdered erythritol, divided
- 2 teaspoons vanilla extract

Directions:

1. Whisk together ½ cup of the powdered erythritol and water in a saucepan over medium heat until it starts to darken. Divide the mixture among six small ramekins and set aside to cool.
2. Combine the coconut milk and cream in a saucepan and cook over medium heat until it starts to steam, then whisk in the rest of the erythritol, vanilla extract and salt. Beat the eggs in a mixing bowl then pour a few tablespoons of the warmed milk into it while whisking.
3. Pour the egg mixture into the milk mixture and whisk smooth, then pour into the ramekins.
4. Cover the ramekins with foil and place them in the steamer insert in your Instant Pot. Pour in ½ cup water, then close and lock the lid.
5. Press the Manual button and adjust the timer for 9 minutes.
6. When the timer goes off, let the pressure vent naturally, then press Cancel.
7. When the pot has depressurized, open the lid.

8. Remove the ramekins and let the flan cool to room temperature then chill until ready to serve.

Nutrition:
calories 205 fat 19.5g ,protein 4.5g ,carbs 3g ,fiber 1g ,net carbs 2g

Blueberry Mug Cake

Prep Time + Cook time:15 minutes , Servings: 4
Ingredients:
- 4 large eggs
- ½ cup fresh blueberries
- 1 cup of water

What you'll need from the store cupboard:
- ¼ teaspoon salt
- 1 1/3 cup almond flour
- 2 teaspoons vanilla extract
- ¼ cup sugar-free maple syrup

Directions:
1. Place the trivet in the Instant Pot and add 1 cup of water.
2. Whisk together the almond flour, egg, sugar-free maple syrup, vanilla, and salt in a mixing bowl.
3. Fold in the blueberries then divide the mixture among four 8-ounce jars.
4. Cover the jars with foil, then place on the trivet, close and lock the lid.
5. Press the Manual button and adjust the timer to 10 minutes.
6. When the timer goes off, do a Quick Release by pressing Cancel and switching the steam valve to "venting."
7. When the pot has depressurized, open the lid.
8. Remove the jars and let them cool a little before serving.

Nutrition:
calories 285 fat 23g ,protein 14g ,carbs 9.5g ,fiber 4g ,net carbs 5.5g

Classic Crème Brulee

Prep Time + Cook time:14 minutes , Servings: 6
Ingredients:
- 6 large egg yolks
- 2 tablespoons granular erythritol

What you'll need from the store cupboard:
- 2 cups heavy cream
- 3 tablespoons powdered erythritol
- 1 tablespoon vanilla extract
- 1 cup water

Directions:
1. Whisk together the heavy cream, egg yolks, powdered erythritol, and the vanilla in a bowl.
2. Divide the mixture among 6 small ramekins and cover with foil.
3. Place the steamer rack in the Instant Pot and add 1 cup water.
4. Place the ramekins in the steamer rack, offsetting the stacks so they are stable.
5. Close and lock the lid, then press the Manual button and adjust the timer to 9 minutes.
6. When the timer goes off, let the pressure vent for 15 minutes then do a Quick Release by pressing Cancel and switching the steam valve to "venting."
7. When the pot has depressurized, open the lid.
8. Remove the ramekins and chill until they are cold.
9. Sprinkle the granular erythritol over the crème brulees and place under the broiler until browned.
10. Let the topping harden before serving.

Nutrition:
calories 200 fat 19g ,protein 3.5g ,carbs 2g ,fiber 0g ,net carbs 2g

Ricotta Lemon Cheesecake

Prep Time + Cook time:40 minutes , Servings: 6

Ingredients:

- 1/3 cup whole-milk ricotta cheese
- 2 large eggs
- 2 cups of water

What you'll need from the store cupboard:

- 1 (8-ounce) package cream cheese, softened
- ¼ cup powdered erythritol
- Juice and zest of 1 lemon
- ½ teaspoon lemon extract

Directions:

1. Combine all of the ingredients except the eggs in a mixing bowl.
2. Beat until the mixture is smooth then adjust erythritol to taste.
3. Lower the mixer speed and blend in the eggs until they are fully incorporated, being careful not to overmix.
4. Grease a 6-inch springform pan and pour in the cheesecake mixture.
5. Cover the pan with foil and place it in the Instant Pot on top of the trivet.
6. Pour in 2 cups of water, then close and lock the lid.
7. Press the Manual button and adjust the timer for 30 minutes on High Pressure.
8. When the timer goes off, let the pressure vent naturally.
9. When the pot has depressurized, open the lid.
10. Let the cheesecake cool a little then chill for at least 8 hours before serving.

Nutrition:

calories 180 fat 16g ,protein 6.5g ,carbs 2g ,fiber 0g ,net carbs 2g

Creamy Lemon Curd

Prep Time + Cook time:20 minutes , Servings: 6

Ingredients:

- 2 large eggs
- 2 large egg yolks

What you'll need from the store cupboard:

- 3 ounces butter
- 2/3 cup lemon juice
- 1 cup powdered erythritol

Directions:

1. Combine the butter and erythritol in a mixing bowl and beat for 2 minutes.
2. Whisk together the eggs and yolks then drizzle them into the bowl while mixing.
3. Add the lemon juice and mix until well combined.
4. Divide the mixture among three half-pint jars and loosely cover with the lids.
5. Place the jars in the Instant Pot on the trivet then pour in 1 ½ cups water.
6. Close and lock the lid.
7. Press the Manual button and adjust the timer to 10 minutes on High Pressure.
8. When the timer goes off, let the pressure vent for 10 minutes then do a Quick Release by pressing Cancel and switching the steam valve to "venting."
9. When the pot has depressurized, open the lid.
10. Let the curd thicken for 20 minutes at room temperature then chill.

Nutrition:

calories 150 fat 15g ,protein 3g ,carbs 1g ,fiber 0g ,net carbs 1g

Chocolate Pudding Cake

Prep Time + Cook time:14 minutes , Servings: 8

Ingredients:

- 2/3 cup stevia-sweetened dark chocolate
- ½ cup unsweetened applesauce
- 2 large eggs

What you'll need from the store cupboard:

- ½ cup almond flour
- 1 teaspoon vanilla extract
- ¼ cup unsweetened cocoa powder

Directions:

1. Melt the chocolate in a double boiler over low heat until melted.
2. In a mixing bowl, whisk together the applesauce, eggs, and vanilla extract.
3. Whisk in the almond flour and cocoa powder, then stir in the melted chocolate.
4. Pour the mixture into a greased 6-inch cake pan.
5. Place the pan in the Instant Pot on top of the trivet and pour in 2 cups of water.
6. Close and lock the lid.
7. Press the Manual button and adjust the timer on High Pressure for 4 minutes.
8. When the timer goes off, do a Quick Release by pressing Cancel and switching the steam valve to "venting."
9. When the pot has depressurized, open the lid.
10. Remove the pan and let the cake cool 10 minutes before removing it.

Nutrition:

calories 150 fat 11g ,protein 5g ,carbs 16.5g ,fiber 5g ,net carbs 11.5g

Mini Vanilla Custards

Prep Time + Cook time:29 minutes , Servings: 4

Ingredients:

- 2 tablespoons water
- 1 cup unsweetened almond milk
- 3 large eggs

What you'll need from the store cupboard:

- Pinch salt
- 1 cup heavy cream
- ¾ cup powdered erythritol, divided
- 1 tablespoon vanilla extract

Directions:

1. Whisk together ½ cup of the powdered erythritol and water in a saucepan over medium heat until the erythritol melts.
2. Divide the mixture among four small ramekins and set aside to cool.
3. Combine the almond milk and cream in a saucepan and cook over medium heat until it starts to steam, then whisk in the rest of the erythritol, vanilla extract and salt.
4. Beat the eggs in a mixing bowl.
5. Whisk a few tablespoons of the milk mixture into the eggs, then whisk in the rest in a steady stream.
6. Cover the ramekins with foil and place them in the steamer insert in your Instant Pot.
7. Pour in ½ cup water, then close and lock the lid.
8. Press the Manual button and adjust the timer for 9 minutes.
9. When the timer goes off, let the pressure vent naturally, then press Cancel.
10. When the pot has depressurized, open the lid.
11. Remove the ramekins and let the custards cool for 10 minutes then serve warm.

Nutrition:

calories 175 fat 16g ,protein 5.5g ,carbs 2g ,fiber 0.5g ,net carbs 1.5g

Coconut Almond Cake

Prep Time + Cook time:45 minutes , Servings: 8

Ingredients:

- ½ cup unsweetened shredded coconut
- 2 large eggs

What you'll need from the store cupboard:

- ½ cup heavy cream
- ¼ cup butter, melted
- 1 cup almond flour
- 6 tablespoons powdered erythritol
- 1 teaspoon baking powder
- 2 cups of water

Directions:

1. Whisk together the almond flour, coconut, erythritol, and baking powder in a mixing bowl.
2. Add the eggs, heavy cream, and butter then whisk smooth.
3. Pour into a greased 6-inch cake pan and cover with foil.
4. Place the steamer rack in the Instant Pot and add 2 cups of water.
5. Put the cake pan on the steamer rack, then close and lock the lid.
6. Press the Manual button and adjust the timer to 40 minutes at High Pressure.
7. When the timer goes off, let the pressure vent for 10 minutes then do a Quick Release by pressing Cancel and switching the steam valve to "venting."
8. When the pot has depressurized, open the lid.
9. Remove the cake and let it cool in the pan for 15 minutes before turning out.

Nutrition:

calories 290 fat 27.5g ,protein 5.5g ,carbs 7g ,fiber 3.5g ,net carbs 3.5g

Easy Chocolate Cheesecake

Prep Time + Cook time:40 minutes , Servings: 6

Ingredients:

- 1/3 cup whole-milk ricotta cheese
- 2 large eggs

What you'll need from the store cupboard:

- 1 (8-ounce) package cream cheese, softened
- ¼ cup powdered erythritol
- 1 teaspoon vanilla extract
- ¼ cup unsweetened cocoa powder

Directions:

1. Combine all of the ingredients except the eggs in a mixing bowl.
2. Beat until the mixture is smooth then adjust erythritol to taste.
3. Lower the mixer speed and blend in the eggs until they are fully incorporated, being careful not to overmix.
4. Grease a 6-inch springform pan and pour in the cheesecake mixture.
5. Cover the pan with foil and place it in the Instant Pot on top of the trivet.
6. Pour in 2 cups of water, then close and lock the lid.
7. Press the Manual button and adjust the timer for 30 minutes on High Pressure.
8. When the timer goes off, let the pressure vent naturally.
9. When the pot has depressurized, open the lid.
10. Let the cheesecake cool a little then chill for at least 6 hours before serving.

Nutrition:

calories 180 fat 16g ,protein 6.5g ,carbs 3.5g .fiber 1g ,net carbs 2.5g

21-Day Meal Plan for Keto Journey

This is a sample 21-day meal plan, if you like this meal plan, you can follow it, if you don't like it, you can make your own meal plan, but make sure obey the keto diet rules, don't take too much calories one day and keep the nutrition balance.

DAY 1

Breakfast: Mexican Egg Casserole
Lunch: Easy Lemon Pepper Salmon
Dinner: Easy Beef Bourguignon
Side Dish: Spaghetti Squash

DAY 2

Breakfast: Sausage and Broccoli Egg Casserole
Lunch: Shrimp Bisque
Dinner: Shredded Beef
Side Dish: Garlic Asparagus

DAY 3

Breakfast: Sausage Gravy
Lunch: Shrimp Scampi
Dinner: Braised Beef Short Ribs
Side Dish: Garlic Green Beans

DAY 4

Breakfast: Eggs and Tomatoes with Avocado
Lunch: Coconut Fish Curry
Dinner: Classic Meatloaf
Side Dish: Lemon Parmesan Zucchini "Noodles"

DAY 5

Breakfast: Sausage and Broccoli Egg Casserole
Lunch: Ginger Soy Salmon
Dinner: Korean BBQ Beef
Side Dish: Buffalo Chicken Soup

DAY 6

Breakfast:Cheesy Paprika Broccoli and Scallions
Lunch: Steamed Mussels
Dinner: Bolognese Sauce
Side Dish: Creamy Mashed Cauliflower

DAY 7

Breakfast: Cheesy Broccoli Cake
Lunch: Lemon Tilapia Packets
Dinner: Stewed Beef with Mushrooms
Side Dish: Spaghetti Squash

DAY 8

Breakfast: Creamy Cinnamon Coconut Mix
Lunch: Steamed Crab Legs
Dinner: Beef and Chorizo Chili
Side Dish: Easy Taco Chicken Soup

DAY 9

Breakfast: Easy Eggs in a Jar
Lunch: Coconut Shrimp
Dinner: Quick and Easy Taco Meat
Side Dish: Buffalo Chicken Soup

DAY 10

Breakfast: Eggs and Tomatoes with Avocado
Lunch: Chili Lime Salmon
Dinner: Balsamic Beef Pot Roast
Side Dish: Hearty Beef and Bacon Chili

DAY 11

Breakfast: Cheesy Cauliflower and Ham Casserole
Lunch: Indian Butter Chicken
Dinner: Balsamic Pork Tenderloin
Side Dish: Buffalo Chicken Soup

DAY 12

Breakfast: Cheesy Broccoli Cake
Lunch: Turkey-Stuffed Peppers
Dinner: Easy Lamb with Gravy
Side Dish: Clam and Cauliflower Chowder

DAY 13

Breakfast: Easy Spinach and Tomato Frittata
Lunch: Garlic Soy-Glazed Chicken
Dinner: Spicy Pork Carnitas
Side Dish: Garlic Green Beans

DAY 14

Breakfast: Cheesy Cauliflower and Ham Casserole
Lunch: Italian Turkey Breast with Gravy
Dinner: Braised Lamb Chops
Side Dish: Garlic Asparagus

DAY 15

Breakfast: Bacon, Cheese, and Veggie Egg Bake
Lunch: Whole Roasted Chicken
Dinner: Ginger Soy-Glazed Pork Tenderloin
Side Dish: Clam and Cauliflower Chowder

DAY 16

Breakfast: Sausage and Broccoli Egg Casserole
Lunch: Italian Chicken Stew
Dinner: Herb-Roasted Lamb Shoulder
Side Dish: Buffalo Chicken Soup

DAY 17

Breakfast: Avocado Tussle with White Mushrooms
Lunch: Chicken Cacciatore
Dinner: Curried Pork Shoulder
Side Dish: Spaghetti Squash

DAY 18

Breakfast: Sausage Gravy
Lunch: Stewed Chicken and Kale
Dinner: Curried Lamb Stew
Side Dish: Lemon Parmesan Zucchini "Noodles"

DAY 19

Breakfast: Cheddar, Ham, and Chive Egg Cups
Lunch: Lemon Garlic Chicken
Dinner: Smothered Pork Chops
Side Dish: Garlic Asparagus

DAY 20

Breakfast: Easy Spinach and Tomato Frittata
Lunch: Creamy Salsa Chicken
Dinner: Rosemary Garlic Leg of Lamb
Side Dish: Clam and Cauliflower Chowder

DAY 21

Breakfast: Cheesy Broccoli Cake
Lunch: Chili Lime Salmon
Dinner: Easy Beef Bourguignon
Side Dish: Clam and Cauliflower Chowder

Appendix 1 Measurement Conversion Charts

Volume Equivalents(Liquid)

US STANDARD	US STANDARD(OUNCES)	METRIC(APPROXIMATE)
2 TABLESPOONS	1 fl.oz.	30 mL
1/4 CUP	2 fl.oz.	60 mL
1/2 CUP	4 fl.oz.	120 mL
1 CUP	8 fl.oz.	240 mL
1 1/2 CUP	12 fl.oz.	355 mL
2 CUPS OR 1 PINT	16 fl.oz.	475 mL
4 CUPS OR 1 QUART	32 fl.oz.	1 L
1 GALLON	128 fl.oz.	4 L

Volume Equivalents (DRY)

US STANDARD	METRIC (APPROXIMATE)
1/8 TEASPOON	0.5 mL
1/4 TEASPOON	1 mL
1/2 TEASPOON	2 mL
3/4 TEASPOON	4 mL
1 TEASPOON	5 mL
1 TABLESPOON	15 mL
1/4 CUP	59 mL
1/2 CUP	118 mL
3/4 CUP	177 mL
1 CUP	235 mL
2 CUPS	475 mL
3 CUPS	700 mL
4 CUPS	1 L

Weight Equivalents

US STANDARD	METRIC (APPROXIMATE)
1/2 OUNCE	15g
1 OUNCE	30g
2 OUNCE	60g
4 OUNCE	115g
8 OUNCE	225g
12 OUNCE	340g
16 OUNCES OR 1 POUND	455g

Temperatures Equivalents

FAHRENHEIT (F)	CELSIUS(C) (APPROXIMATE)
250	121
300	149
325	163
350	177
375	190
400	205
425	218
450	232

Appendix 2 Recipes Index